Maths — No Problem!

Singapore Maths
English National Curriculum 2014

Consultant and Author
Dr. Yeap Ban Har

UK Consultant
Dr. Anne Hermanson

Authors
Dr. Foong Pui Yee
Lim Li Gek Pearlyn
Wong Oon Hua

Published by Maths — No Problem!
Copyright © 2016 by Maths — No Problem!

Printed in the United Kingdom
First Printing, 2014
Reprinted twice in 2015 and twice in 2016

ISBN 978-1-910504-02-4

Maths — No Problem!
Dowding House, Coach & Horses Passage
Tunbridge Wells, UK TN2 5NP
www.mathsnoproblem.co.uk

Acknowledgements

This Maths — No Problem! series, adapted from the New Syllabus
Primary Mathematics series, is published in collaboration with
Shing Lee Publishers. Pte Ltd.

Design and Illustration by Kin

Preface

Maths — No Problem! is a comprehensive series that adopts a spiral design with carefully built-up mathematical concepts and processes adapted from the maths mastery approaches used in Singapore. The Concrete-Pictorial-Abstract (C-P-A) approach forms an integral part of the learning process through the materials developed for this series.

Maths — No Problem! incorporates the use of concrete aids and manipulatives, problem-solving and group work.

In Maths — No Problem! Primary 2, these features are exemplified throughout the chapters:

Chapter Opener

Familiar events or occurrences that serve as an introduction for pupils.

In Focus

Includes questions related to various lesson objectives as an introductory activity for pupils.

Count in tens.
10 ones = 1 ten

Let's Learn

Introduces new concepts through a C-P-A approach with the use of engaging pictures and manipulatives. Guided examples are provided for reinforcement.

Activity Time

Provides pupils with opportunities to work as individuals or in small groups to explore mathematical concepts or to play games.

Guided Practice

Comprises questions for further consolidation and for the immediate evaluation of pupils' learning.

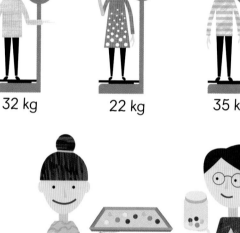

32 kg   22 kg   35 kg

Mind Workout

Challenging non-routine questions for pupils to apply relevant heuristics and to develop higher-order thinking skills.

Maths Journal

Provides pupils with opportunities to show their understanding of the mathematical concepts learnt.

Self Check

Allows pupils to assess their own learning after each chapter.

Self Check

I know how to...

☐ read a thermometer.
☐ measure and write down the temperature.

Contents

How many crayons
are there altogether?

Chapter 1
Numbers to 100

Counting to 100

In Focus

How many crayons are there?

Group them in tens.

Let's Learn

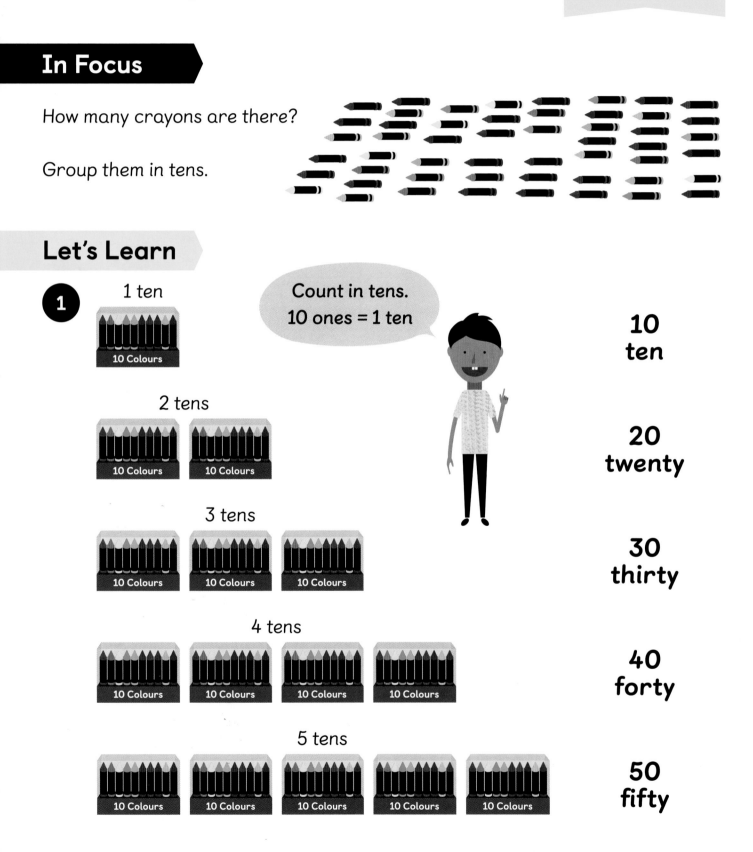

1

1 ten
10 Colours

2 tens
10 Colours 10 Colours

3 tens
10 Colours 10 Colours 10 Colours

4 tens
10 Colours 10 Colours 10 Colours 10 Colours

5 tens
10 Colours 10 Colours 10 Colours 10 Colours 10 Colours

Count in tens.
10 ones = 1 ten

10
ten

20
twenty

30
thirty

40
forty

50
fifty

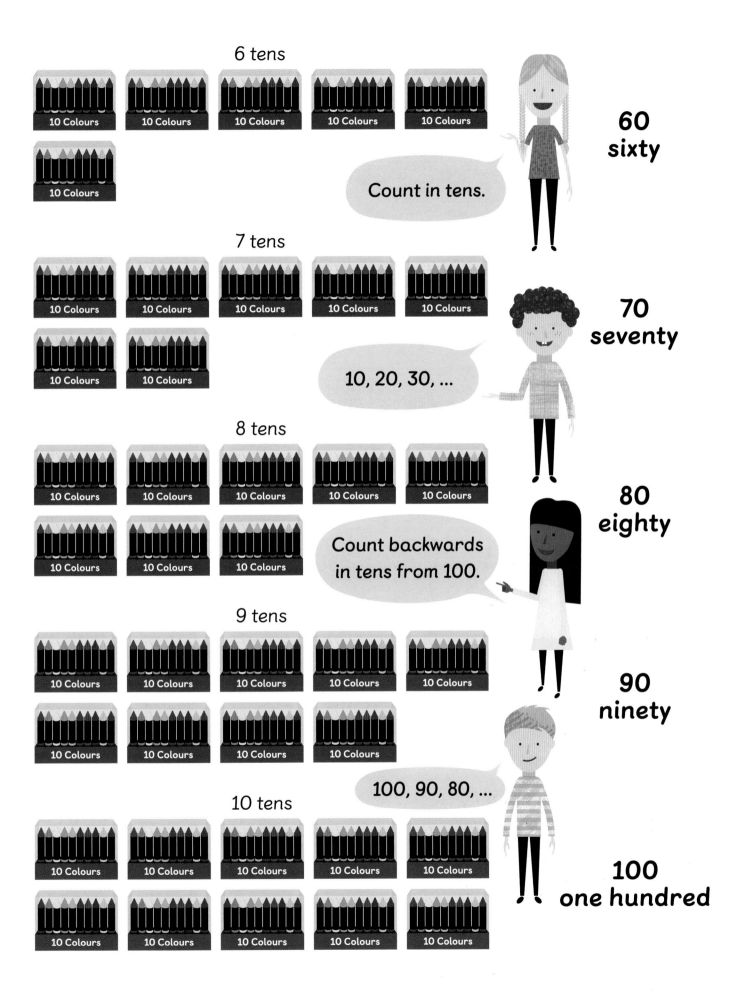

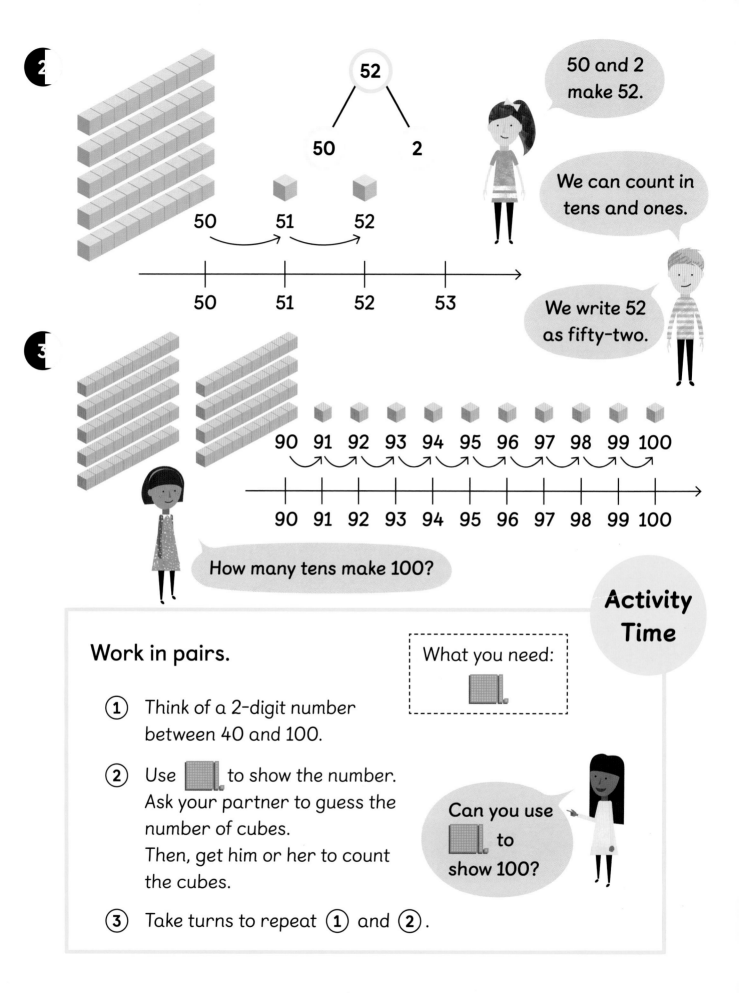

Guided Practice

1 Count.
Write in numbers.

(a)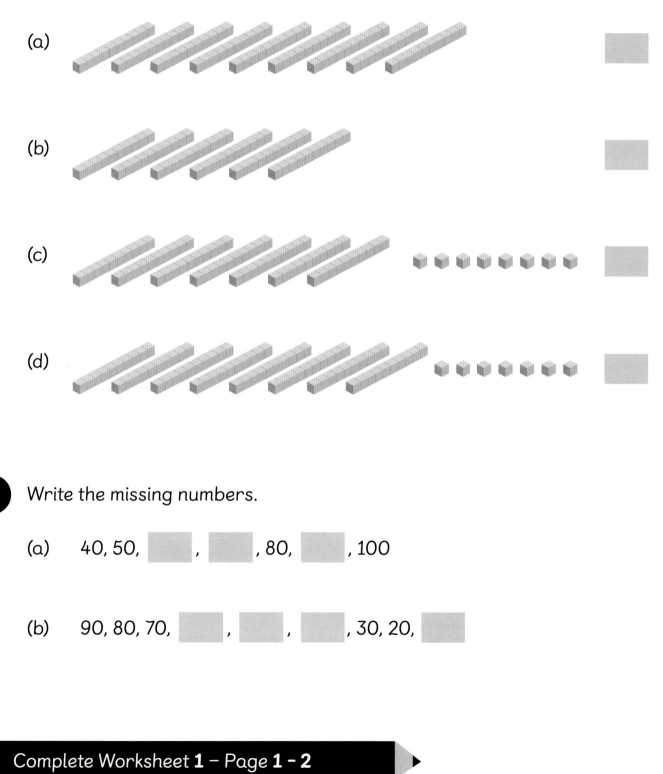

(b)

(c)

(d)

2 Write the missing numbers.

(a)   40, 50, ___ , ___ , 80, ___ , 100

(b)   90, 80, 70, ___ , ___ , ___ , 30, 20, ___

Complete Worksheet 1 – Page 1 - 2

Place Value

In Focus

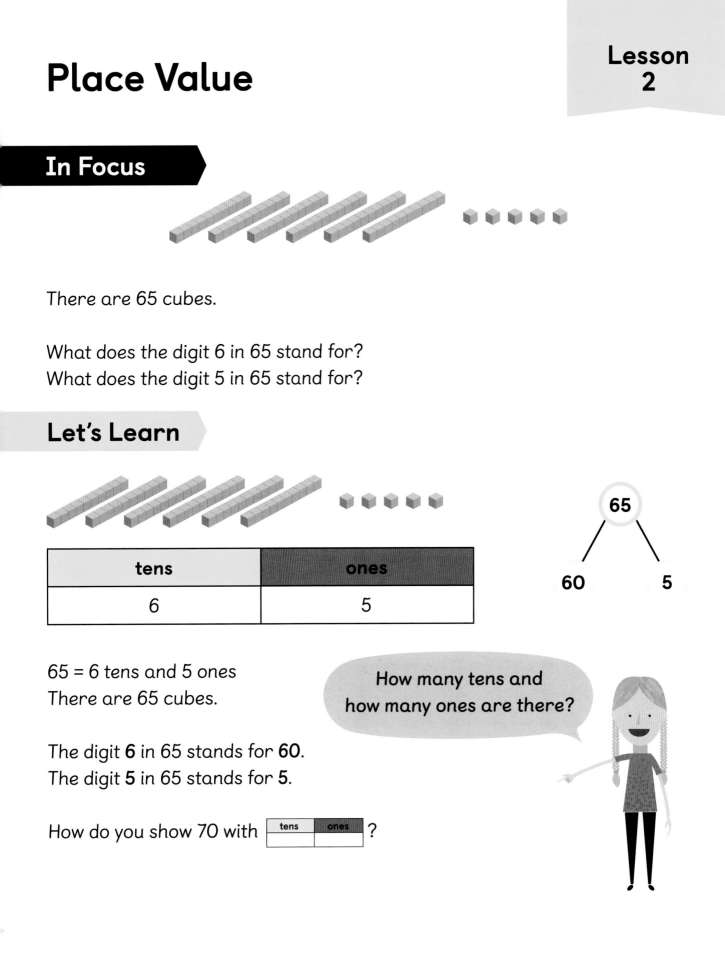

There are 65 cubes.

What does the digit 6 in 65 stand for?
What does the digit 5 in 65 stand for?

Let's Learn

tens	ones
6	5

65

60   5

65 = 6 tens and 5 ones
There are 65 cubes.

How many tens and
how many ones are there?

The digit **6** in 65 stands for **60**.
The digit **5** in 65 stands for **5**.

How do you show 70 with | tens | ones | ?

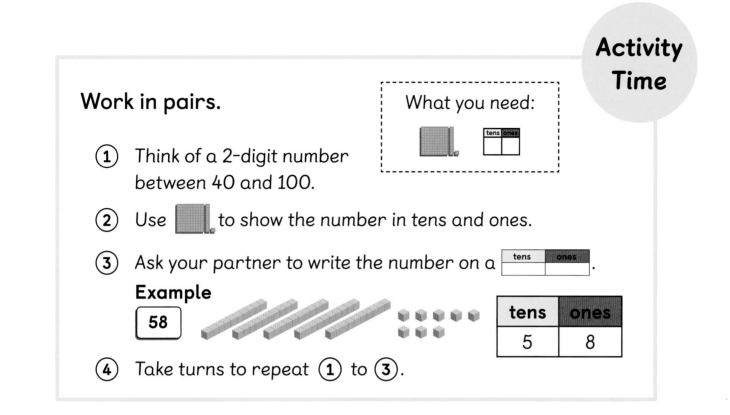

Work in pairs.

① Think of a 2-digit number between 40 and 100.

What you need:

② Use ▦ to show the number in tens and ones.

③ Ask your partner to write the number on a | tens | ones | .

Example

| 58 |

tens	ones
5	8

④ Take turns to repeat ① to ③.

Guided Practice

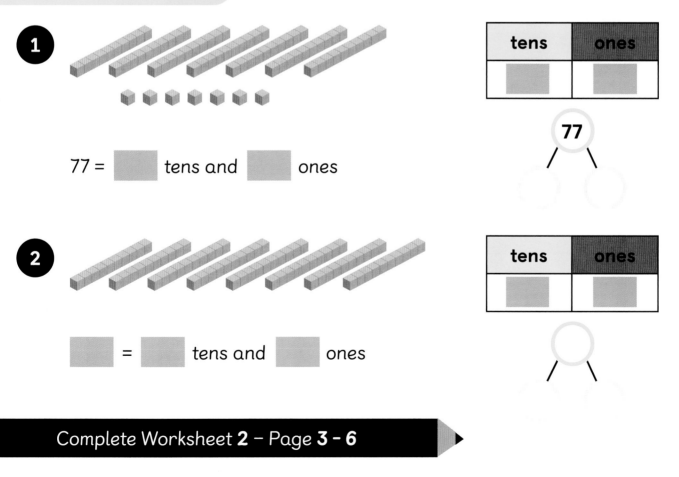

1

77 = ▭ tens and ▭ ones

tens	ones

77

2

▭ = ▭ tens and ▭ ones

tens	ones

Complete Worksheet **2** – Page **3 - 6**

Comparing Numbers

In Focus

Sam   Ruby   Charles

Who has the greatest number of coins?
Who has the smallest number of coins?

Let's Learn

Compare the number of coins.

Ruby

Sam

Charles

tens	ones
7	5

75 = 7 tens and 5 ones

tens	ones
6	3

63 = 6 tens and 3 ones

tens	ones
6	9

69 = 6 tens and 9 ones

Compare the number of tens.

Both 63 and 69 have 6 tens. What should we compare next?

7 tens is more than 6 tens.
75 is more than 63.
75 is more than 69.
75 is the greatest.

3 ones is less than 9 ones.
63 is less than 69.
63 is the smallest.

75 > 63

63 < 69

75 ☐ 69

Is it < or >?

We can arrange the numbers in order.

75,   **69,**   **63**

greatest ⟶ smallest

63,   **69,**   **75**

smallest ⟶ greatest

Play in groups of 3 to 4.

What you need: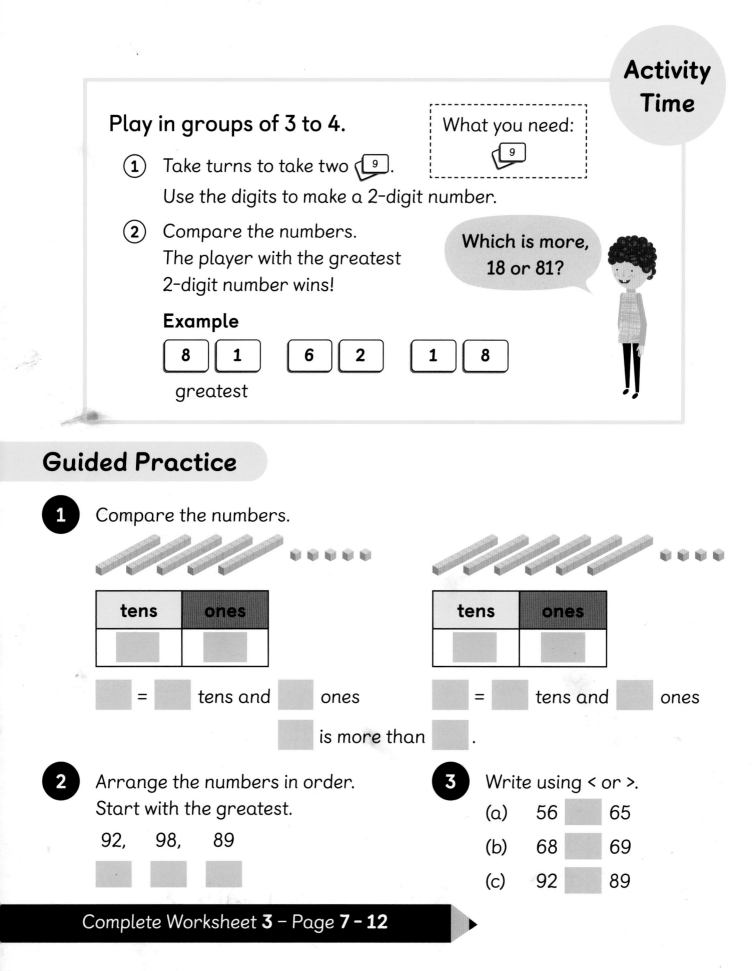

① Take turns to take two 9.
Use the digits to make a 2-digit number.

② Compare the numbers.
The player with the greatest
2-digit number wins!

Which is more, 18 or 81?

Example

| 8 | 1 | | 6 | 2 | | 1 | 8 |

greatest

Guided Practice

1 Compare the numbers.

tens	ones

☐ = ☐ tens and ☐ ones

tens	ones

☐ = ☐ tens and ☐ ones

☐ is more than ☐.

2 Arrange the numbers in order.
Start with the greatest.

92, 98, 89

☐ ☐ ☐

3 Write using < or >.

(a) 56 ☐ 65

(b) 68 ☐ 69

(c) 92 ☐ 89

Complete Worksheet **3** – Page **7 – 12** ▶

Number Bonds

In Focus

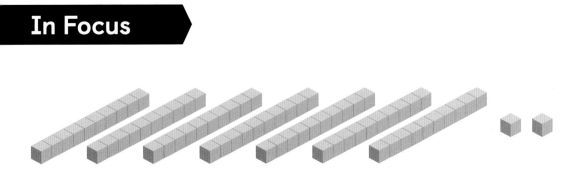

There are 72 cubes.

What does the digit 2 in 72 stand for?
What does the digit 7 in 72 stand for?

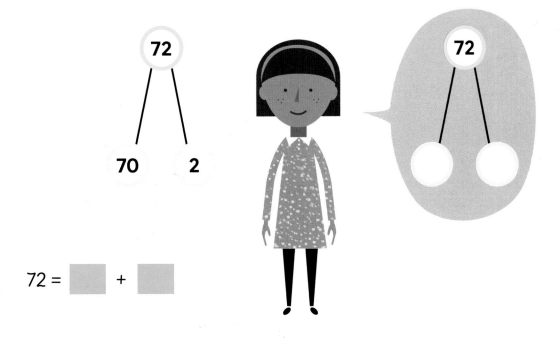

72 = ▢ + ▢

Let's Learn

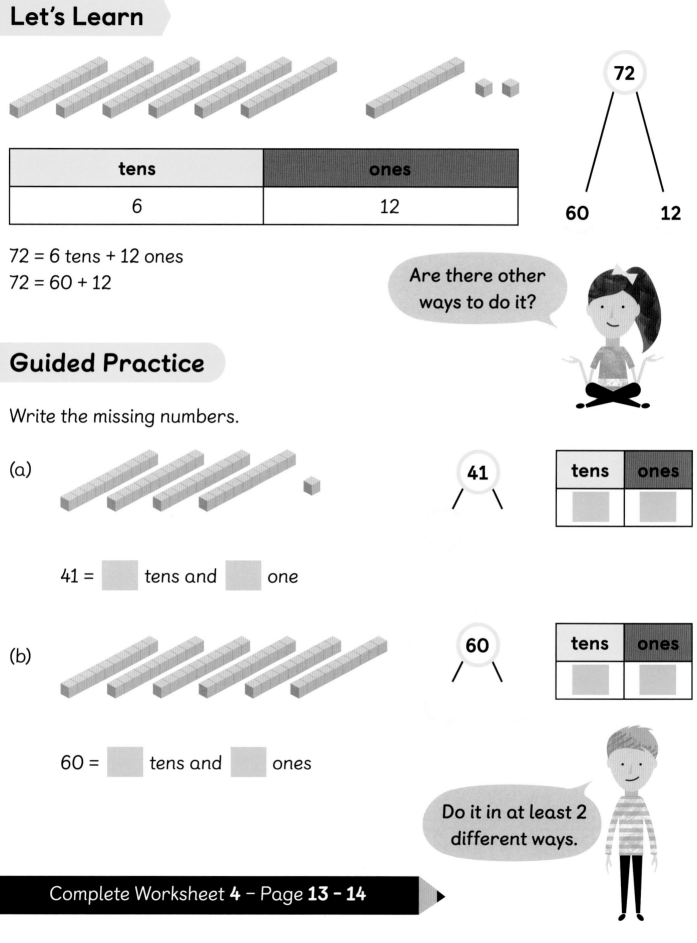

tens	ones
6	12

72 = 6 tens + 12 ones
72 = 60 + 12

72
60   12

Are there other ways to do it?

Guided Practice

Write the missing numbers.

(a)

41

tens	ones

41 = ☐ tens and ☐ one

(b)

60

tens	ones

60 = ☐ tens and ☐ ones

Do it in at least 2 different ways.

Complete Worksheet 4 – Page **13 - 14**

Number Patterns

In Focus

1	2	3	4	5	6	7	8	9	10
11	12	13	14	15	16	17	18	19	20
21	22	23	24	25	26	27	28	29	30
31	32	33	34	35	36	37	38	39	40
41	42	43	44	45	46	47	48	49	50
51	52	53	54	55	56	57	58	59	60
61	62	63	64	65	66	67	68	69	70
71	72	73	74	75	76	77	78	79	80
81	82	83	84	85	86	87	88	89	90
91	92	93	94	95	96	97	98	99	100

This is a one hundred chart.

Look at the numbers in the yellow boxes.
What number patterns do you see?

Let's Learn

1 What is 2 more than 42?

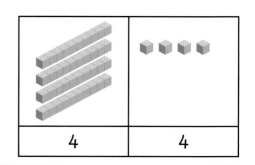

2 more than 42 is 44.

We can make a number pattern. Each number is 2 more than the number before it.

2 more	2 more	2 more	2 more

42	44	46	48	50

41 42 43 44 45 46 47 48 49 50 51

2 What is 2 less than 49?

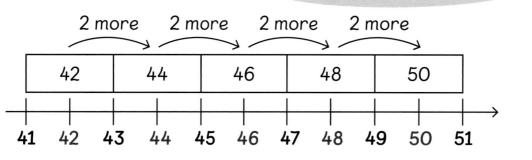

2 less than 49 is 47.

We can make a number pattern. Each number is ___ less than the number before it.

2 less	2 less	2 less	2 less

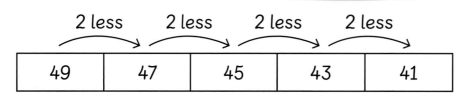

49	47	45	43	41

3 What is 10 more than 40?

(4 tens)	
4	0

10 more →

(5 tens)	
5	0

10 more than 40 is 50.

> We can make a number pattern from 10 to 100.
> Each number is ▢ more than the number before it.

10   10   10   10   10   10   10   10   10
more more more more more more more more more

| 10 | 20 | 30 | 40 | 50 | 60 | 70 | 80 | 90 | 100 |

10   20   30   40   50   60   70   80   90   100

4 What comes next in the pattern?

| 100 | 90 | 80 | 70 | 60 | 50 | ? |

> Each number is ▢ less than the number before it.

10 less than 50 is ▢ .

The number pattern is 100, 90, 80, 70, 60, 50, ▢ .

Guided Practice

1 Complete the number patterns.

(a)

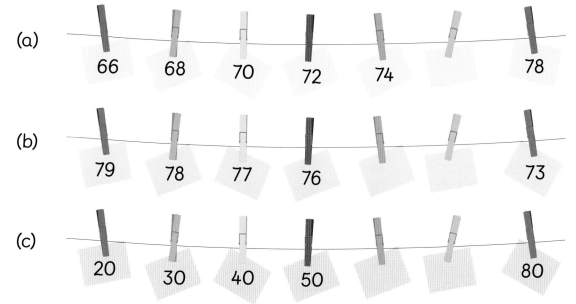

66   68   70   72   74   78

(b)

79   78   77   76   73

(c)

20   30   40   50   80

2 Look at each number pattern and complete it.

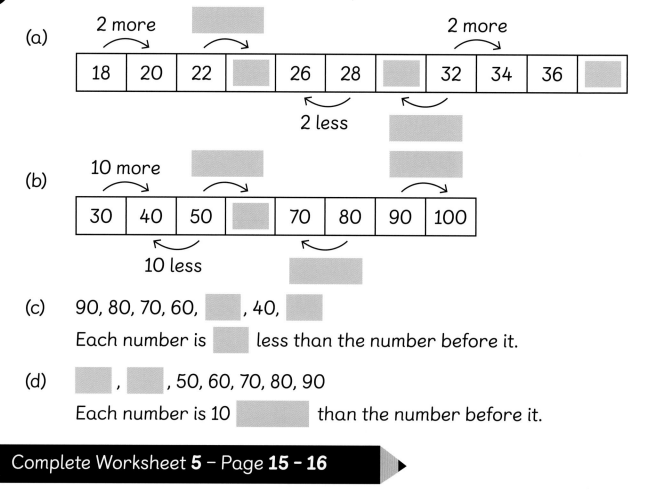

(a)

2 more

| 18 | 20 | 22 | | 26 | 28 | | 32 | 34 | 36 | |

2 more

2 less

(b)

10 more

| 30 | 40 | 50 | | 70 | 80 | 90 | 100 |

10 less

(c)   90, 80, 70, 60, [ ] , 40, [ ]

Each number is [ ] less than the number before it.

(d)   [ ] , [ ] , 50, 60, 70, 80, 90

Each number is 10 [ ] than the number before it.

Complete Worksheet 5 – Page 15 – 16

Number Patterns

In Focus

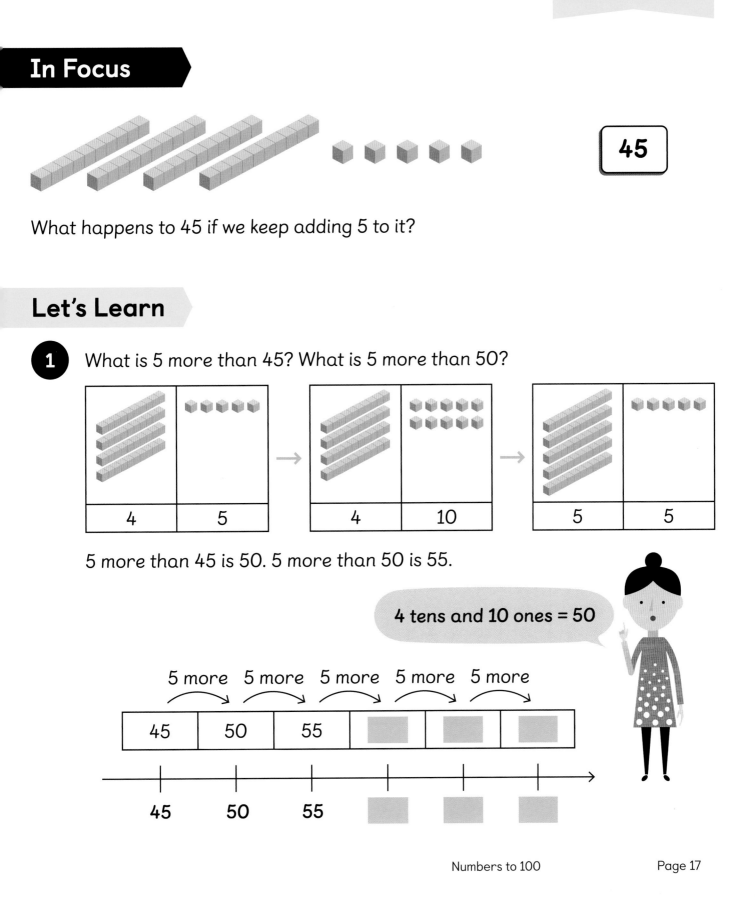

What happens to 45 if we keep adding 5 to it?

Let's Learn

1 What is 5 more than 45? What is 5 more than 50?

5 more than 45 is 50. 5 more than 50 is 55.

4 tens and 10 ones = 50

2 What is 5 less than 45? What is 5 less than 40?

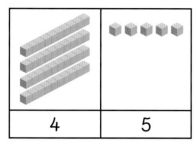 → 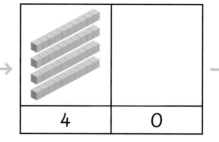 →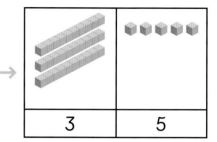

4	5	4	0	3	5

5 less than 45 is 40. 5 less than 40 is 35.

			35	40	45

1	2	3	4	5	6	7	8	9	10
11	12	13	14	15	16	17	18	19	20
21	22	23	24	25	26	27	28	29	30
31	32	33	34	35	36	37	38	39	40
41	42	43	44	45	46	47	48	49	50
51	52	53	54	55	56	57	58	59	60
61	62	63	64	65	66	67	68	69	70
71	72	73	74	75	76	77	78	79	80
81	82	83	84	85	86	87	88	89	90
91	92	93	94	95	96	97	98	99	100

3 What is 3 more than 45? What is 3 more than 48?

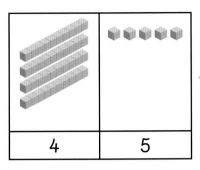 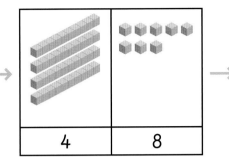 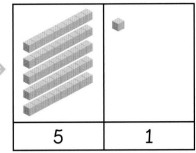

4	5

4	8

5	1

3 more than 45 is 48. 3 more than 48 is 51.

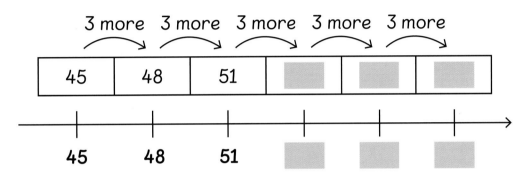

4 What is 3 less than 45? What is 3 less than 42?

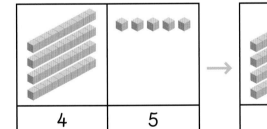 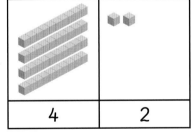 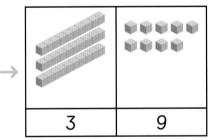

4	5

4	2

3	9

3 less than 45 is 42. 3 less than 42 is 39.

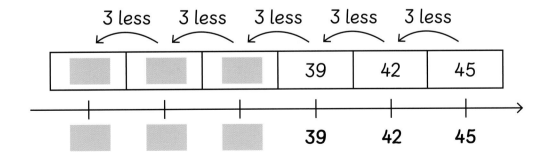

1	2	3	4	5	6	7	8	9	10
11	12	13	14	15	16	17	18	19	20
21	22	23	24	25	26	27	28	29	30
31	32	33	34	35	36	37	38	39	40
41	42	43	44	45	46	47	48	49	50
51	52	53	54	55	56	57	58	59	60
61	62	63	64	65	66	67	68	69	70
71	72	73	74	75	76	77	78	79	80
81	82	83	84	85	86	87	88	89	90
91	92	93	94	95	96	97	98	99	100

Guided Practice

Complete the number patterns.

(a)

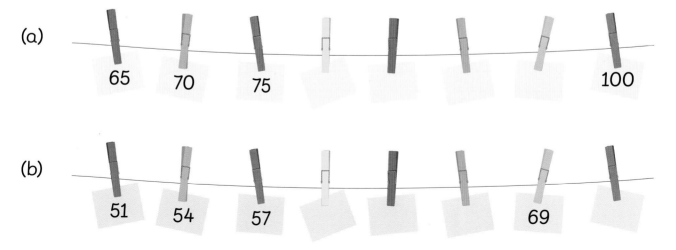

65   70   75   100

(b)

51   54   57   69

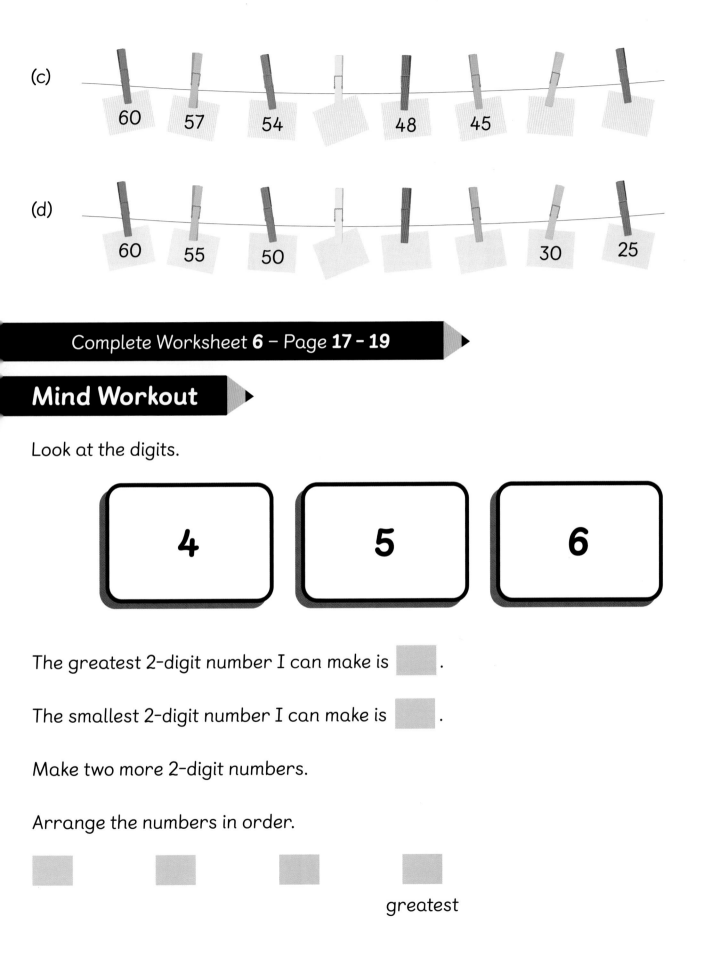

(c)

60   57   54   48   45

(d)

60   55   50   30   25

Complete Worksheet **6** – Page **17 – 19**

Mind Workout

Look at the digits.

| 4 | 5 | 6 |

The greatest 2-digit number I can make is ☐.

The smallest 2-digit number I can make is ☐.

Make two more 2-digit numbers.

Arrange the numbers in order.

☐   ☐   ☐   ☐

greatest

Maths Journal

Do you know that numbers are everywhere?
Look around you for three 2-digit numbers.

You can find 2-digit numbers in
storybooks, around the school,
at home or in your neighbourhood.

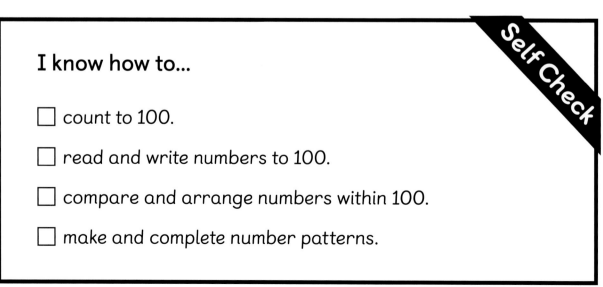

Self Check

I know how to...

☐ count to 100.

☐ read and write numbers to 100.

☐ compare and arrange numbers within 100.

☐ make and complete number patterns.

Chapter 2
Addition and Subtraction

Simple Adding

In Focus

25 + 3 = ?

In what ways can you add?

How many apples are there altogether?

Let's Learn

Add 25 and 3.

Method 1   Count on from 25.

21	22	23	24	25	26	27	28	29	30

25 + 3 = 28

Method 2   Add ones.

2 tens   8 ones

25 + 3 = 28

Method 3   Use 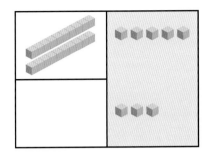 to add.

Step 1   Add the ones.

5 ones + 3 ones = 8 ones

tens	ones
2	5
+	3
	8

Step 2   Add the tens.

tens	ones
2	5
+	3
2	8

25 + 3 = 28

Activity Time

Work in pairs.

Make a correct addition equation.

2 ▢ + ▢ = 2 ▢

Use 3 different digits.

What you need:

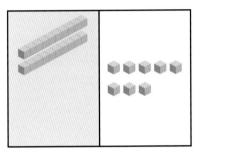

Guided Practice

1   Add 34 and 5. ▢ ◯ ◯

2   7 + 21 = ▢ ◯ ◯

3   27 + 2 = ▢ ◯ ◯

Complete Worksheet 1 · Page **25 – 28**

Simple Adding

In Focus

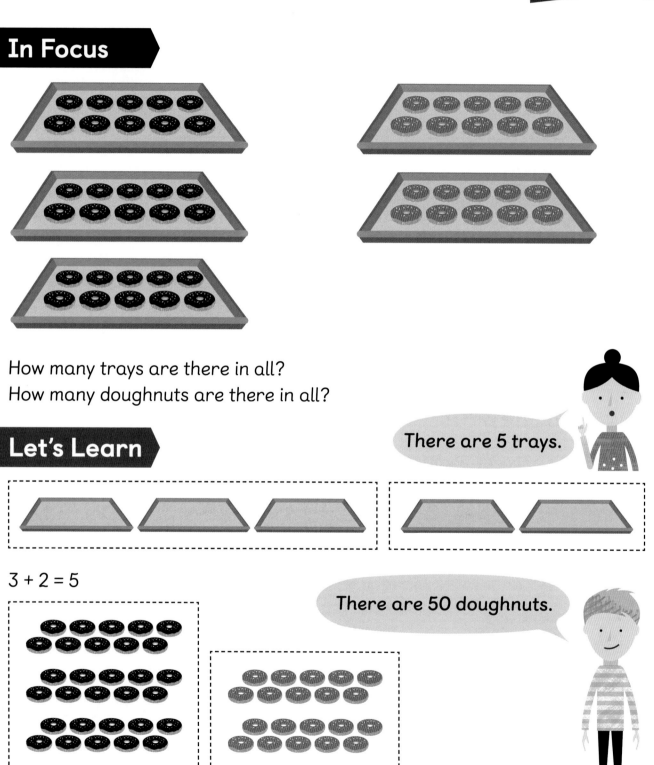

How many trays are there in all?
How many doughnuts are there in all?

Let's Learn

There are 5 trays.

3 + 2 = 5

There are 50 doughnuts.

30 + 20 = 50

Play in pairs.

What you need:

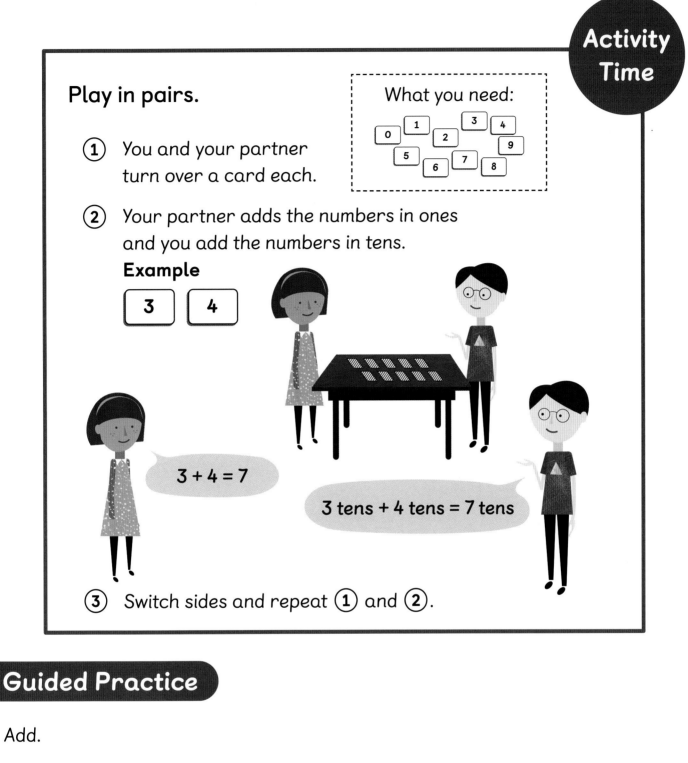

① You and your partner turn over a card each.

② Your partner adds the numbers in ones and you add the numbers in tens.

Example

| 3 | 4 |

3 + 4 = 7

3 tens + 4 tens = 7 tens

③ Switch sides and repeat ① and ②.

Guided Practice

Add.

(a)   2 + 4 = ▢

      20 + 40 = ▢

(b)   9 + 1 = ▢

      90 + 10 = ▢

Complete Worksheet **2** · Page **29 – 32**

Simple Adding

In Focus

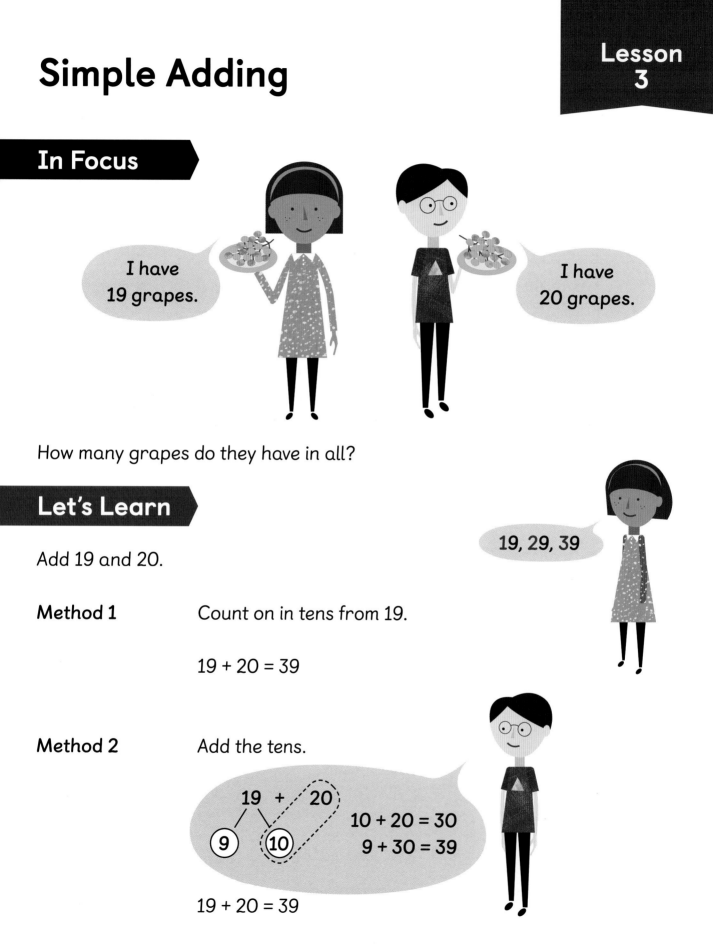

I have 19 grapes.

I have 20 grapes.

How many grapes do they have in all?

Let's Learn

Add 19 and 20.

19, 29, 39

Method 1   Count on in tens from 19.

19 + 20 = 39

Method 2   Add the tens.

19 + 20

9   10

10 + 20 = 30
9 + 30 = 39

19 + 20 = 39

Method 3 Use 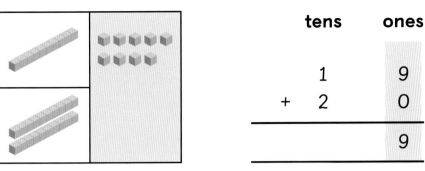 to add.

Step 1   Add the ones.

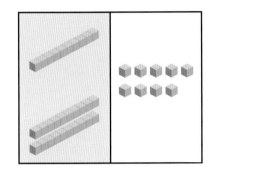

	tens	ones
	1	9
+	2	0
		9

Step 2   Add the tens.
1 ten + 2 tens = 3 tens

	tens	ones
	1	9
+	2	0
	3	9

19 + 20 = 39

Guided Practice

1 Add.

(a)   23 + 10 =

(b)   23 + 20 =

(c)   23 + 30 =

2 Add.

(a)   40 + 36 =

(b)   40 + 25 =

(c)   40 + 17 =

Complete Worksheet 3 • Page 33 – 35

Simple Adding

In Focus

There are 23 oranges in a box.

I am putting in another 14 oranges.

How many oranges are there now?

Let's Learn

Add 23 and 14.

Use [ ] to help you add.

Step 1   Add the ones.
         3 ones + 4 ones = 7 ones

tens	ones
2	3
+ 1	4
	7

3 + 4 = 7

Step 2 Add the tens.

2 tens + 1 ten = 3 tens

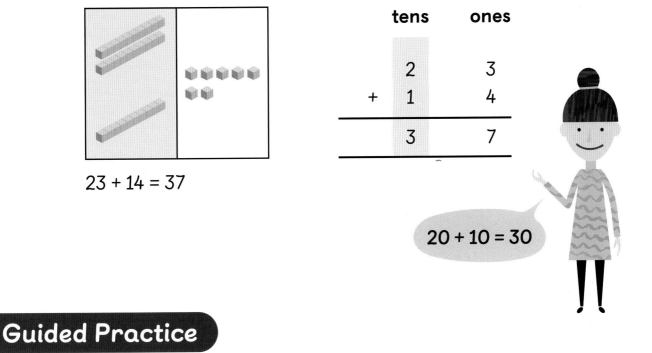

$23 + 14 = 37$

	tens	ones
	2	3
+	1	4
	3	7

20 + 10 = 30

Guided Practice

1 Add.

(a) 17 + 21 =

(b) 24 + 15 =

2 Add.

(a) 22 + 17 =

	tens	ones
	2	2
+	1	7

(b) 31 + 42 =

	tens	ones
	3	1
+	4	2

Complete Worksheet **4** • Page **36 – 39**

Adding with Renaming

In Focus

Hannah has 24 crayons.
Charles has 7 crayons.

How many crayons do they have altogether?

How can we find out?

Let's Learn

Add 24 and 7.

Step 1   Add the ones.
4 ones + 7 ones = 11 ones
Regroup the ones.
11 ones = 1 ten and 1 one

Use [ ] to help you add.

tens	ones
2	4
+	7
1	1

Step 2   Add the tens.
          1 ten + 2 tens = 3 tens

	tens	ones
	2	4
+		7
	1	1
+	2	0
	3	1

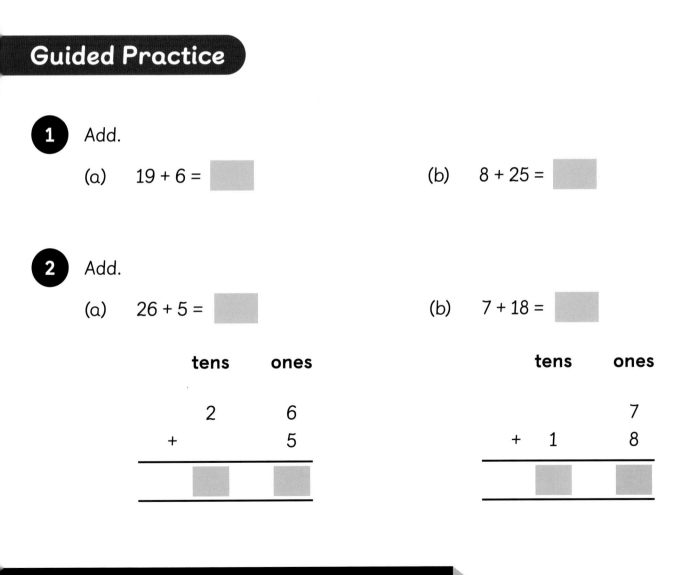

24 + 7 = 31

Guided Practice

1 Add.

(a)   19 + 6 = [ ]

(b)   8 + 25 = [ ]

2 Add.

(a)   26 + 5 = [ ]

	tens	ones
	2	6
+		5
	[ ]	[ ]

(b)   7 + 18 = [ ]

	tens	ones
		7
+	1	8
	[ ]	[ ]

Complete Worksheet **5** · Page **40 – 41**

Adding with Renaming

In Focus

How many cupcakes are there now?

Let's Learn

Add 15 and 18.

Use [blank] to help you add.

Step 1 Add the ones.
5 ones + 8 ones = 13 ones
Regroup the ones.
13 ones = 1 ten and 3 ones

	tens	ones
	1	5
+	1	8
	1	3

Step 2 Add the tens.
1 ten + 1 ten + 1 ten = 3 tens

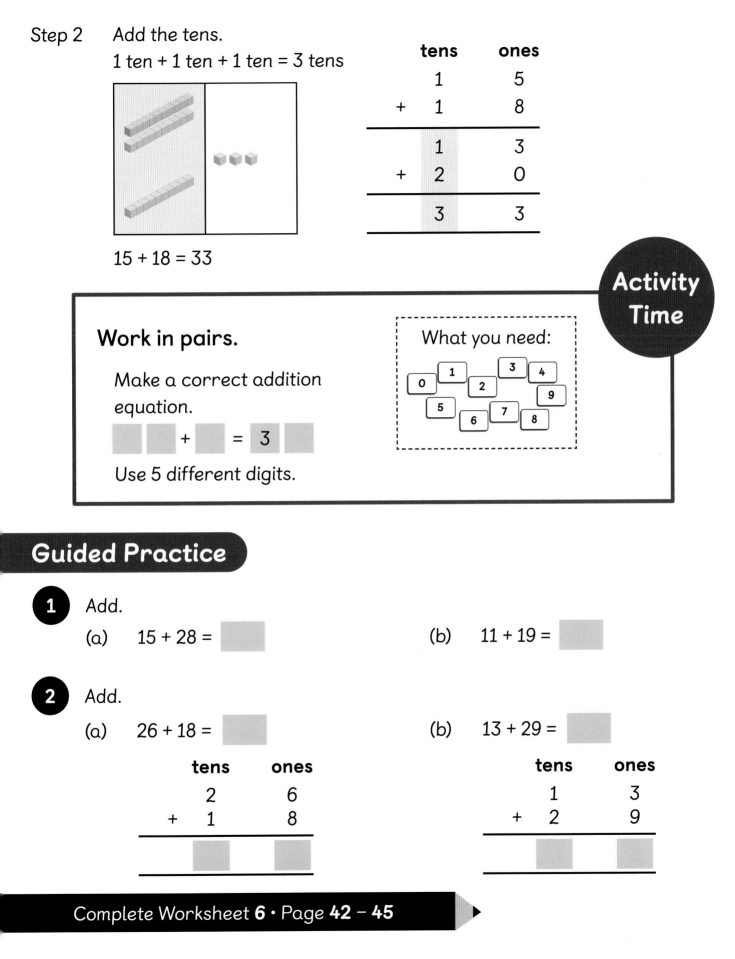

	tens	ones
	1	5
+	1	8
	1	3
+	2	0
	3	3

15 + 18 = 33

Activity Time

Work in pairs.

Make a correct addition equation.

▢ ▢ + ▢ = 3 ▢

Use 5 different digits.

What you need:

0 1 2 3 4 5 6 7 8 9

Guided Practice

1 Add.

(a) 15 + 28 = ▢

(b) 11 + 19 = ▢

2 Add.

(a) 26 + 18 = ▢

	tens	ones
	2	6
+	1	8
	▢	▢

(b) 13 + 29 = ▢

	tens	ones
	1	3
+	2	9
	▢	▢

Complete Worksheet **6** · Page **42 – 45**

Simple Subtracting

In Focus

How many balloons are there left?

Let's Learn

Subtract 3 from 28.

Method 1   Count back from 28.

21	22	23	24	25	26	27	28	29	30

28 – 3 = 25

Method 2   Subtract ones.

2 tens   5 ones

28 – 3 = 25

28 – 3

20   8

8 – 3 = 5
20 + 5 = 25

Method 3   Use 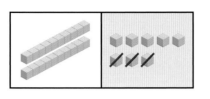 to subtract.

Step 1   Subtract the ones.

8 ones − 3 ones = 5 ones

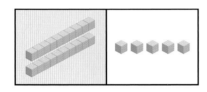

tens	ones
2	8
−	3
	5

Step 2   Subtract the tens.

tens	ones
2	8
−	3
2	5

28 − 3 = 25

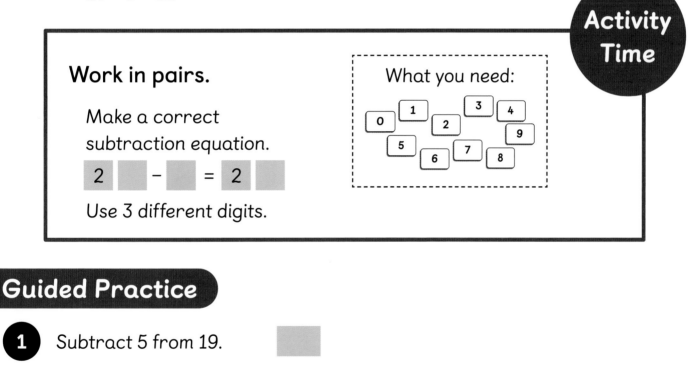

Activity Time

Work in pairs.

Make a correct subtraction equation.

2 ▢ − ▢ = 2 ▢

Use 3 different digits.

What you need:

0   1   3   4
2   9
5   7
6   8

Guided Practice

1 Subtract 5 from 19. ▢

2 Subtract.

(a)   37   −   2   =   ▢

(b)   21   −   0   =   ▢

Complete Worksheet **7** · Page **46 – 49**

Simple Subtracting

In Focus

Amira gives away 1 basket of apples.
How many baskets and apples does she have left?

Let's Learn

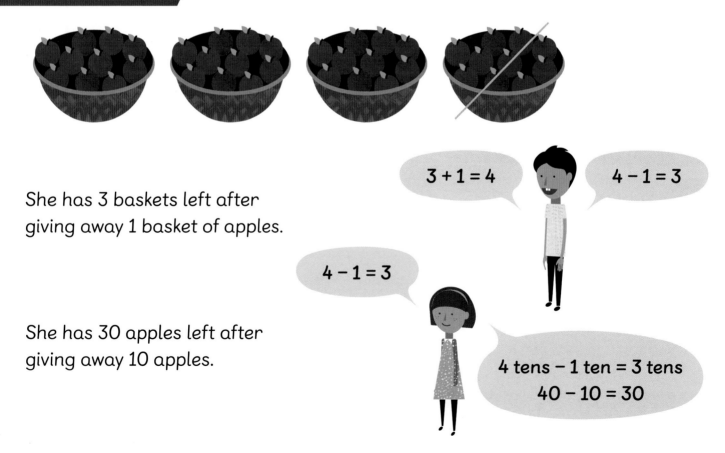

She has 3 baskets left after giving away 1 basket of apples.

$3 + 1 = 4$

$4 - 1 = 3$

$4 - 1 = 3$

She has 30 apples left after giving away 10 apples.

4 tens − 1 ten = 3 tens
$40 - 10 = 30$

Play in pairs.

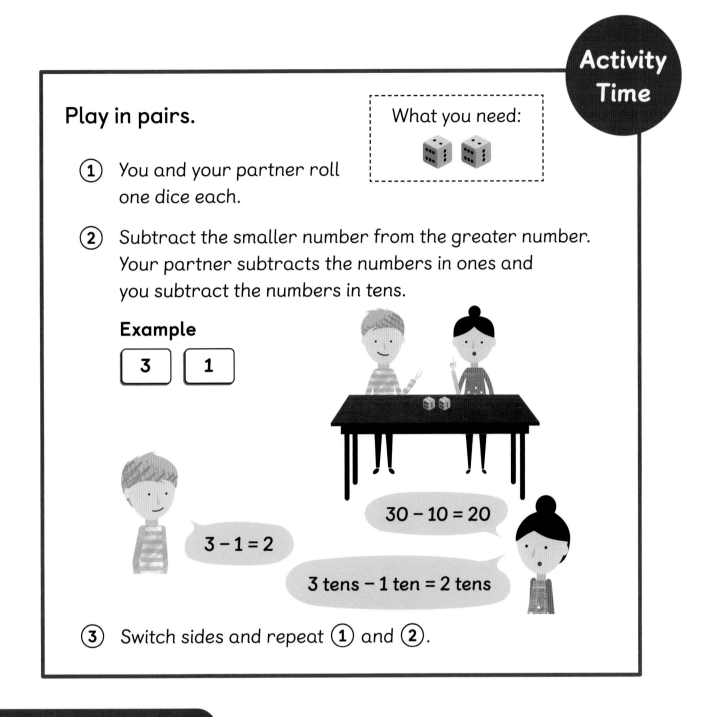

① You and your partner roll one dice each.

② Subtract the smaller number from the greater number. Your partner subtracts the numbers in ones and you subtract the numbers in tens.

Example

| 3 | 1 |

3 − 1 = 2

30 − 10 = 20

3 tens − 1 ten = 2 tens

③ Switch sides and repeat ① and ②.

Guided Practice

Subtract.

(a)   5 − 2 =

    50 − 20 =

(b)   9 − 1 =

    90 − 10 =

Complete Worksheet **8** · Page **50 − 53**

Simple Subtracting

In Focus

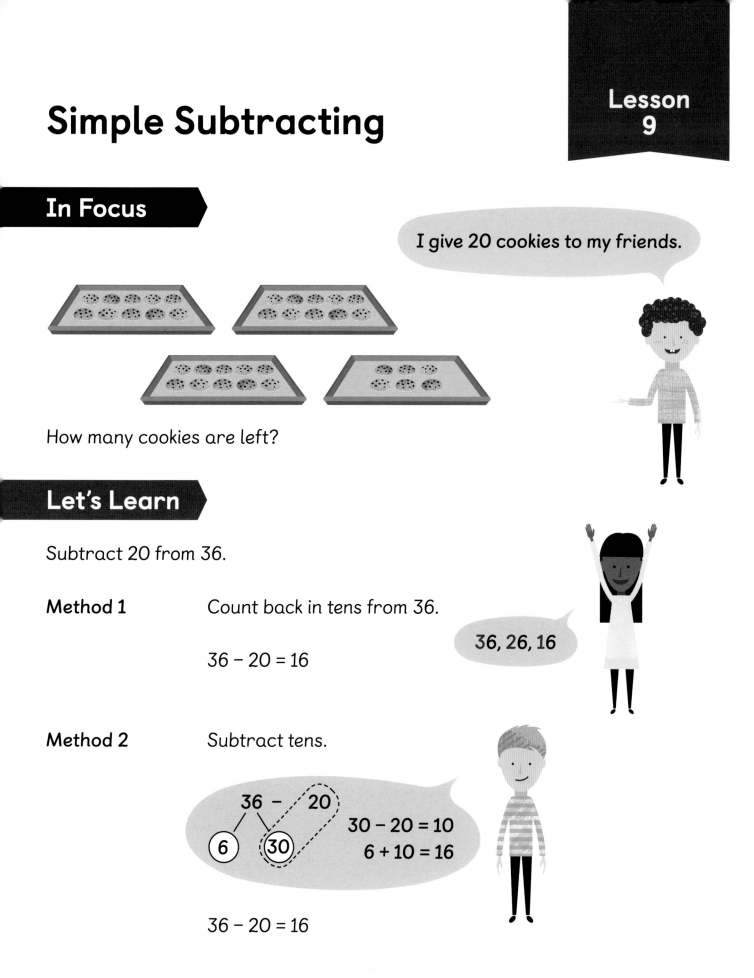

I give 20 cookies to my friends.

How many cookies are left?

Let's Learn

Subtract 20 from 36.

Method 1   Count back in tens from 36.

36, 26, 16

$36 - 20 = 16$

Method 2   Subtract tens.

$36 - 20$

6   30

$30 - 20 = 10$
$6 + 10 = 16$

$36 - 20 = 16$

Method 3 Use 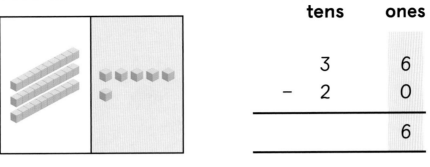 to subtract.

Step 1 Subtract the ones.

	tens	ones
	3	6
−	2	0
		6

Step 2 Subtract the tens.
3 tens − 2 tens = 1 ten

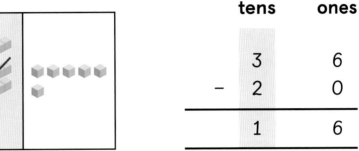

	tens	ones
	3	6
−	2	0
	1	6

36 − 20 = 16

Guided Practice

1 Subtract.

(a) 37 − 10 =

(b) 37 − 20 =

(c) 37 − 30 =

2 Subtract.

(a) 16 − 10 =

(b) 46 − 10 =

(c) 52 − 10 =

Complete Worksheet **9** · Page **54 – 56**

Simple Subtracting

In Focus

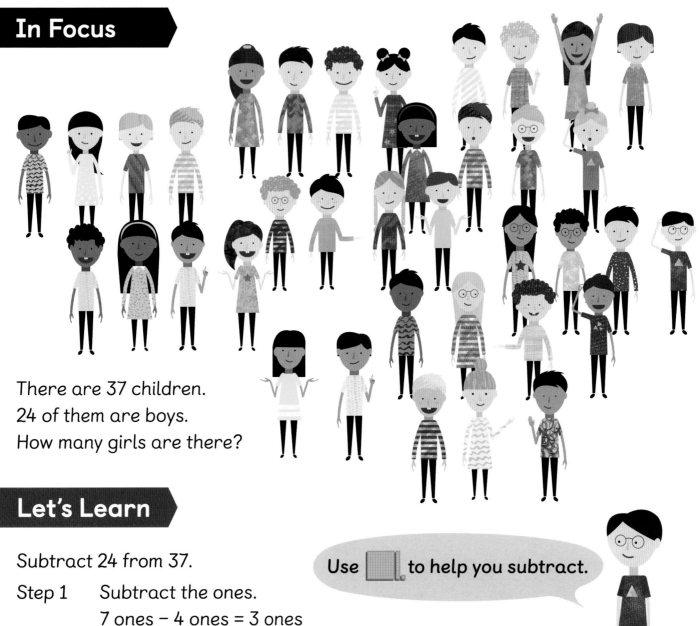

There are 37 children.
24 of them are boys.
How many girls are there?

Let's Learn

Subtract 24 from 37.

Step 1   Subtract the ones.
          7 ones − 4 ones = 3 ones

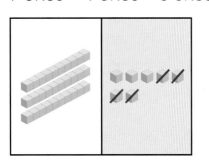

Use [ ] to help you subtract.

tens	ones
3	7
− 2	4
	3

Subtract the tens.
      3 tens – 2 tens = 1 ten

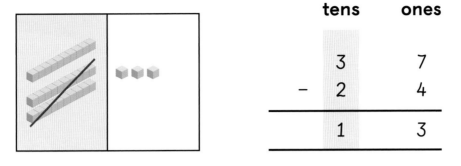

	tens	ones
	3	7
–	2	4
	1	3

37 – 24 = 13

Guided Practice

1   Subtract.

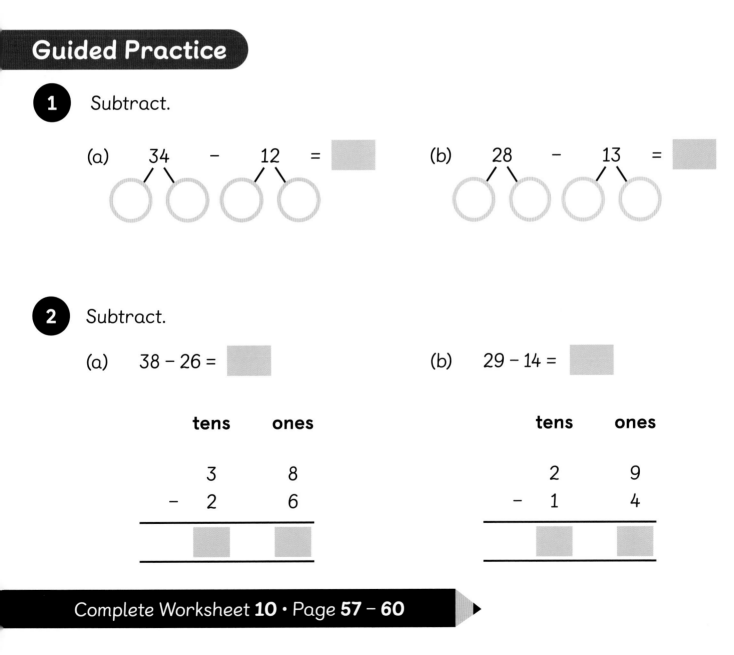

(a)   34   –   12   =

(b)   28   –   13   =

2   Subtract.

(a)   38 – 26 =

(b)   29 – 14 =

	tens	ones
	3	8
–	2	6

	tens	ones
	2	9
–	1	4

Complete Worksheet **10** · Page **57 – 60**

Subtracting with Renaming

In Focus

There are 23 pencils.
5 pencils are removed.
How many pencils are left
in the holder?

Let's Learn

Method 1   Subtract 5 from 10.

23 – 5

13   10

23 – 5 = 18

10 – 5 = 5

5 + 13 = 18

tens	ones
2	3
–	5
2	2

I subtract 3 ones
from 5 ones.

Hannah is
wrong. Why?

Method 2   Use  to subtract.

Step 1   Regroup 1 ten into 10 ones.
Subtract the ones.
13 ones – 5 ones = 8 ones

tens	ones
$\overset{1}{2}$	$\overset{13}{3}$
–	5
	8

13 – 5 = 8

Step 2   Subtract the tens.

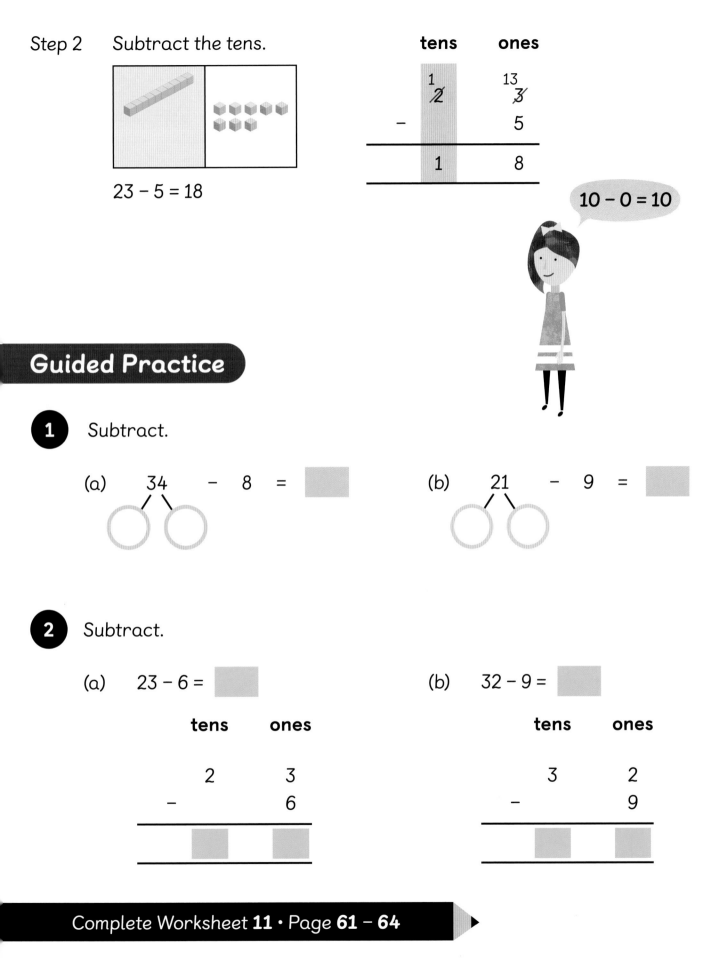

$23 - 5 = 18$

tens	ones
1 $\cancel{2}$	13 $\cancel{3}$
−	5
1	8

10 − 0 = 10

Guided Practice

1 Subtract.

(a)   34   −   8   =

(b)   21   −   9   =

2 Subtract.

(a)   23 − 6 =

tens	ones
2	3
−	6

(b)   32 − 9 =

tens	ones
3	2
−	9

Complete Worksheet **11** · Page **61 – 64**

Subtracting with Renaming

In Focus

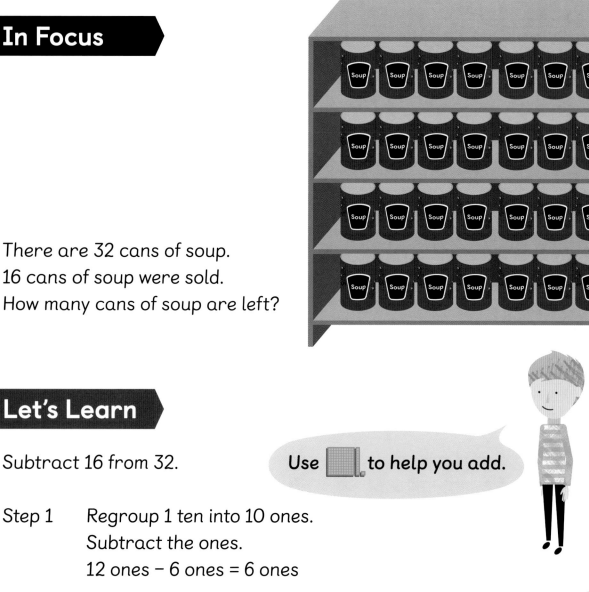

There are 32 cans of soup.
16 cans of soup were sold.
How many cans of soup are left?

Let's Learn

Subtract 16 from 32.

Use  to help you add.

Step 1   Regroup 1 ten into 10 ones.
Subtract the ones.
12 ones − 6 ones = 6 ones

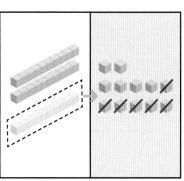

tens	ones
²З	¹²2
− 1	6
	6

12 − 6 = 6

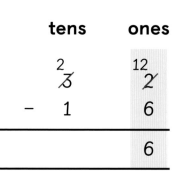

Step 2   Subtract the tens.
2 tens − 1 ten = 1 ten

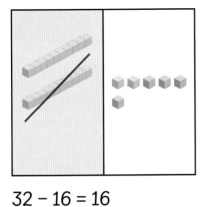

32 − 16 = 16

tens	ones
$\overset{2}{\cancel{3}}$	$\overset{12}{\cancel{2}}$
− 1	6
1	6

20 − 10 = 10

Guided Practice

1 Subtract.

(a)   24   −   16   = ▢

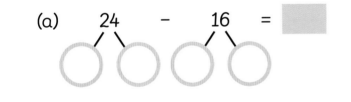

(b)   36   −   19   = ▢

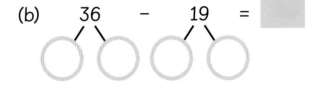

2 Subtract.

(a)   26 − 17 = ▢

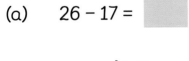

	tens	ones
	▢	▢
−	▢	▢
	▢	▢

(b)   33 − 15 = ▢

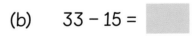

	tens	ones
	▢	▢
−	▢	▢
	▢	▢

Complete Worksheet **12** · Page **65 – 68**

Addition of Three Numbers

In Focus

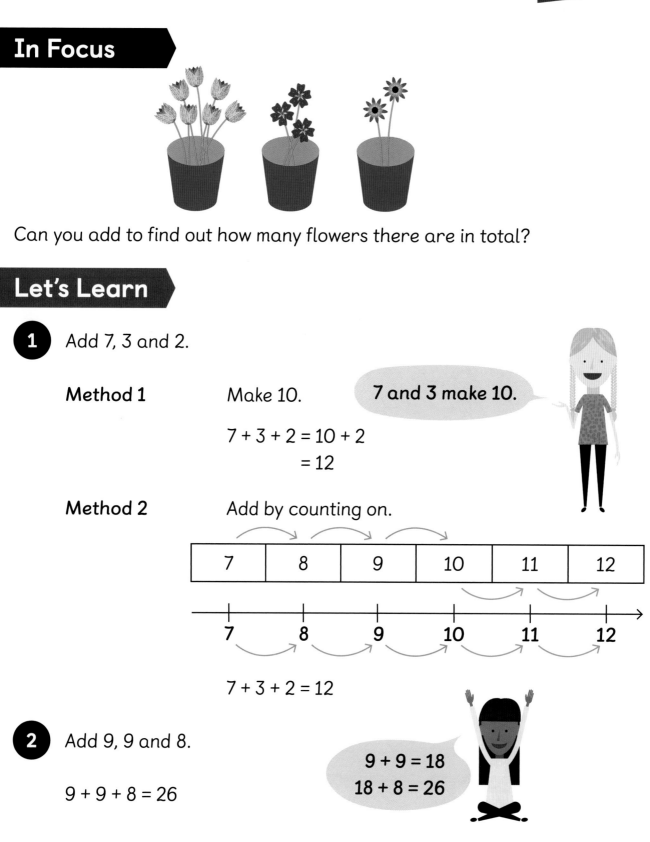

Can you add to find out how many flowers there are in total?

Let's Learn

1 Add 7, 3 and 2.

Method 1   Make 10.

7 and 3 make 10.

$$7 + 3 + 2 = 10 + 2$$
$$= 12$$

Method 2   Add by counting on.

7	8	9	10	11	12

7   8   9   10   11   12

$$7 + 3 + 2 = 12$$

2 Add 9, 9 and 8.

$$9 + 9 + 8 = 26$$

$$9 + 9 = 18$$
$$18 + 8 = 26$$

Guided Practice

1 Make 10 and add.

(a)   2 + 8 + 4 = ☐   + ☐

           = ☐

(b)   3 + 9 + 1 = ☐   + ☐

           = ☐

2 Add.

(a)   6 + 7 + 4 = ☐

(b)   9 + 0 + 4 = ☐

(c)   8 + 5 + 9 = ☐

(d)   7 + 9 + 6 = ☐

Complete Worksheet 13 · Page 69 – 71

Mind Workout

Use 1-digit numbers to complete the addition equation.

Use 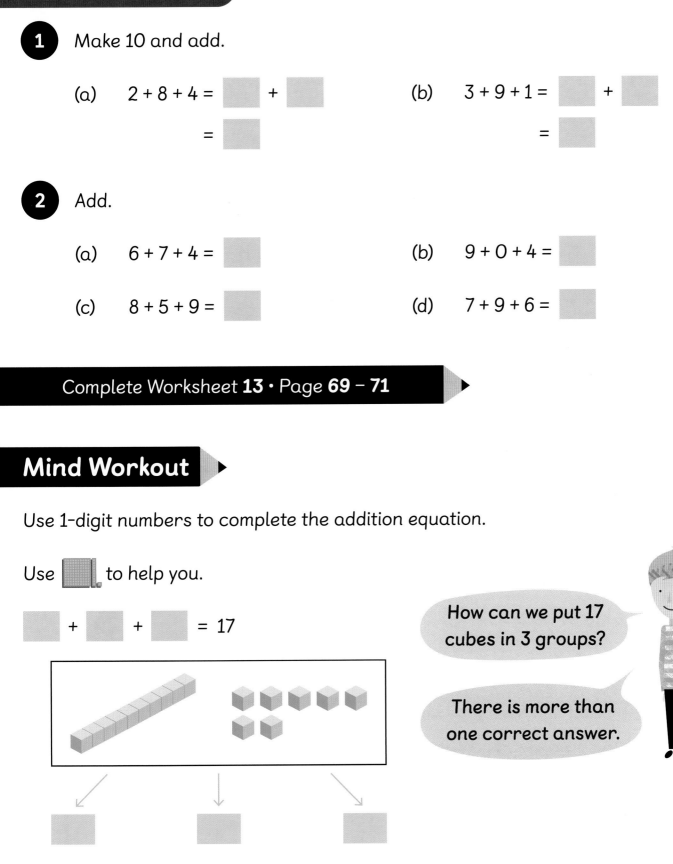 to help you.

☐ + ☐ + ☐ = 17

How can we put 17 cubes in 3 groups?

There is more than one correct answer.

How many pupils are there altogether?
Write down different ways to add.

Which way do you like best?
Why?

Self Check

I know how to...

☐ add numbers without renaming.

☐ add numbers with renaming.

☐ subtract numbers without renaming.

☐ subtract numbers with renaming.

☐ add three numbers.

How many balloons are there altogether?

Chapter 3
Multiplication of 2, 5 and 10

Multiplication as Equal Groups

In Focus

How many cupcakes are there altogether?

Let's Learn

$3 + 3 + 3 + 3 = 12$

4 threes = 12

4 groups of 3 = 12

$4 × 3 = 12$

There are 12 cupcakes altogether.

$4 × 3 = 12$ is read as 4 times 3 equals 12.

There are 4 groups. Each group has 3 cupcakes.

Activity Time

Work in pairs.

What you need:

① Show equal groups using fewer than 30 counters.

Example

$4 + 4 + 4 = 12$

3 fours = 12

3 groups of 4 = 12

$3 × 4 = 12$

② Your partner will count the number of .

③ Switch sides and repeat ① and ②.

Guided Practice

Write the missing numbers.

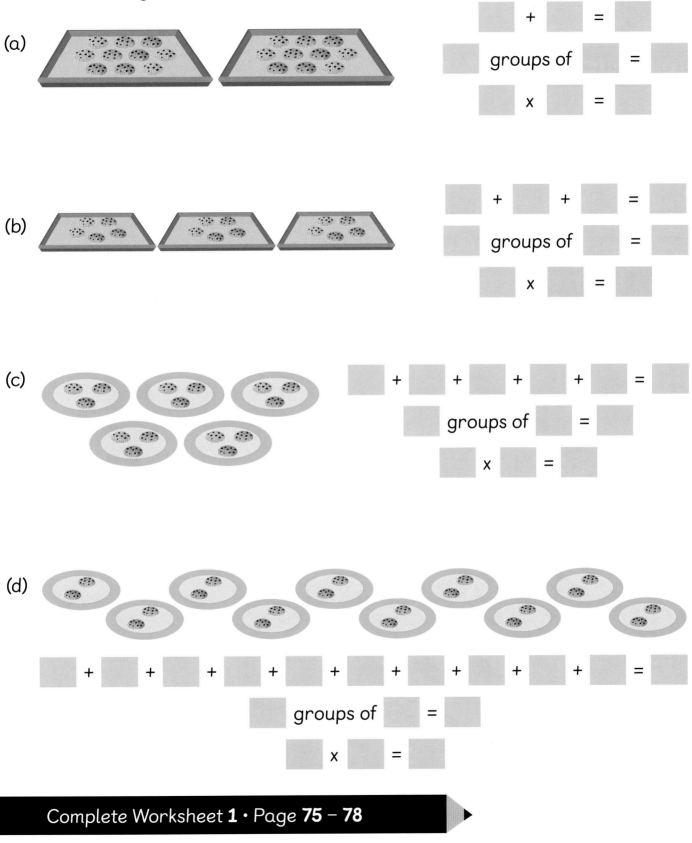

(a)

☐ + ☐ = ☐

☐ groups of ☐ = ☐

☐ x ☐ = ☐

(b)

☐ + ☐ + ☐ = ☐

☐ groups of ☐ = ☐

☐ x ☐ = ☐

(c)

☐ + ☐ + ☐ + ☐ + ☐ = ☐

☐ groups of ☐ = ☐

☐ x ☐ = ☐

(d)

☐ + ☐ + ☐ + ☐ + ☐ + ☐ + ☐ + ☐ = ☐

☐ groups of ☐ = ☐

☐ x ☐ = ☐

Complete Worksheet **1** · Page **75 – 78**

2 Times Table

In Focus

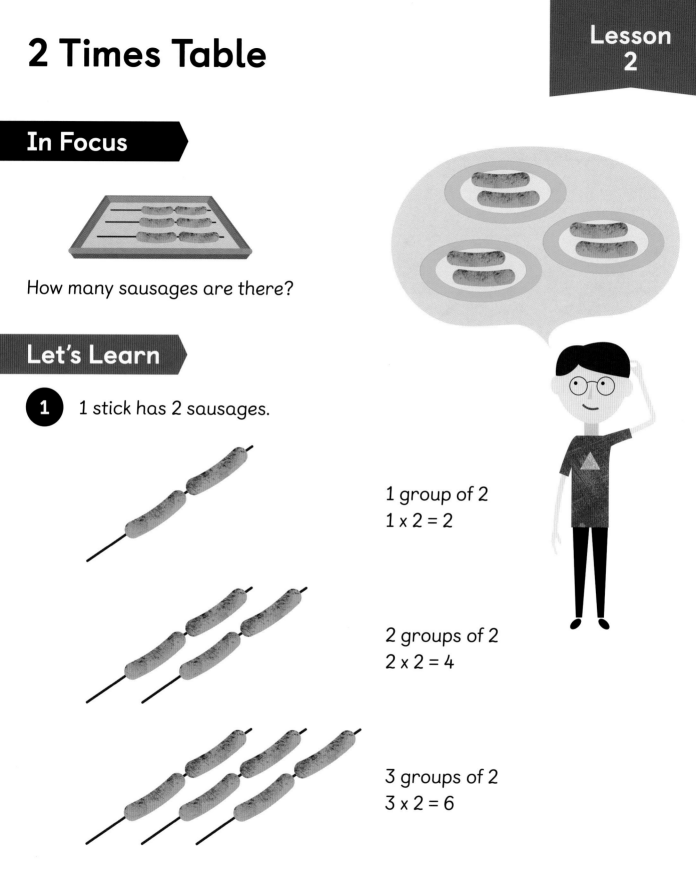

How many sausages are there?

Let's Learn

1 1 stick has 2 sausages.

1 group of 2
1 x 2 = 2

2 groups of 2
2 x 2 = 4

3 groups of 2
3 x 2 = 6

There are 6 sausages altogether.

2 Use 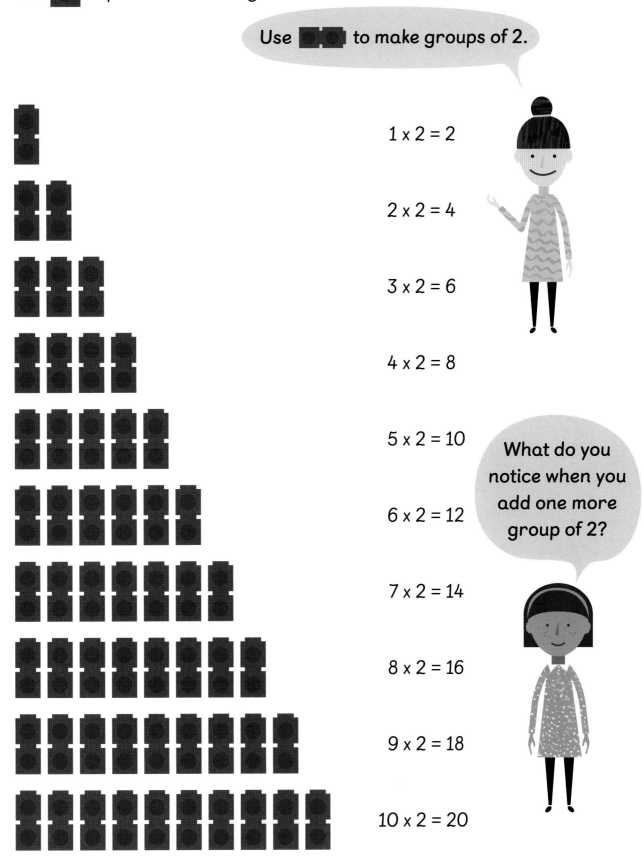 in place of a sausage.

Use to make groups of 2.

1 x 2 = 2

2 x 2 = 4

3 x 2 = 6

4 x 2 = 8

5 x 2 = 10

What do you notice when you add one more group of 2?

6 x 2 = 12

7 x 2 = 14

8 x 2 = 16

9 x 2 = 18

10 x 2 = 20

Guided Practice

1 Complete the multiplication equations.

(a)

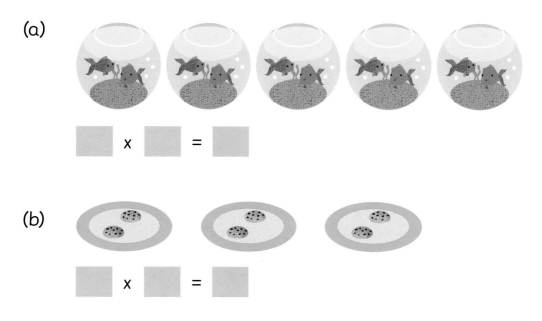

$$\boxed{} \times \boxed{} = \boxed{}$$

(b)

$$\boxed{} \times \boxed{} = \boxed{}$$

2 Complete the multiplication equations.

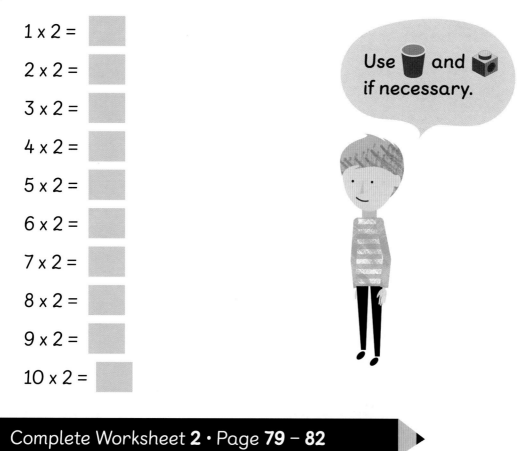

1 x 2 = $\boxed{}$

2 x 2 = $\boxed{}$

3 x 2 = $\boxed{}$

4 x 2 = $\boxed{}$

5 x 2 = $\boxed{}$

6 x 2 = $\boxed{}$

7 x 2 = $\boxed{}$

8 x 2 = $\boxed{}$

9 x 2 = $\boxed{}$

10 x 2 = $\boxed{}$

Use and if necessary.

Complete Worksheet 2 · Page 79 – 82

2 Times Table

In Focus

There are 10 bags of cupcakes.
Each bag has 2 cupcakes.
How many cupcakes are there altogether?

Let's Learn

2, 4, 6, 8, 10, 12, 14, 16, 18, 20

1 Count in twos.

2   4   6   8   10   12   14   16   18   20

1	2	3	4	5	6	7	8	9	10
11	12	13	14	15	16	17	18	19	20

There are 20 cupcakes altogether.

What number pattern do you see on the number chart?

2   6 x 2 = ▢

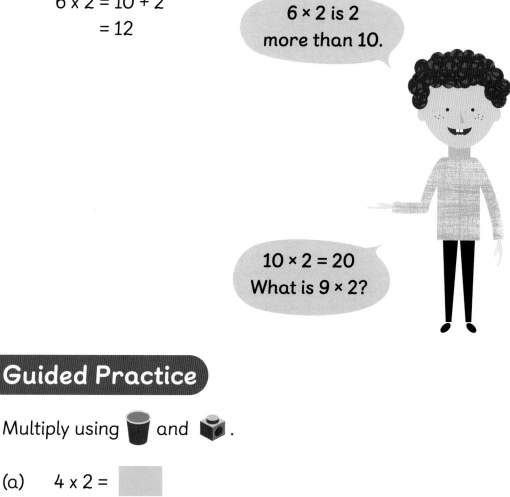

5 x 2 = 10

6 x 2 = 10 + 2

       = 12

6 × 2 is 2 more than 10.

10 × 2 = 20
What is 9 × 2?

Guided Practice

Multiply using 🥤 and 🧊 .

(a)   4 x 2 = ▢

(b)   9 x 2 = ▢

Complete Worksheet 3 • Page 83 – 84

5 Times Table

What is the total number of marshmallows?

1 1 stick has 5 marshmallows.

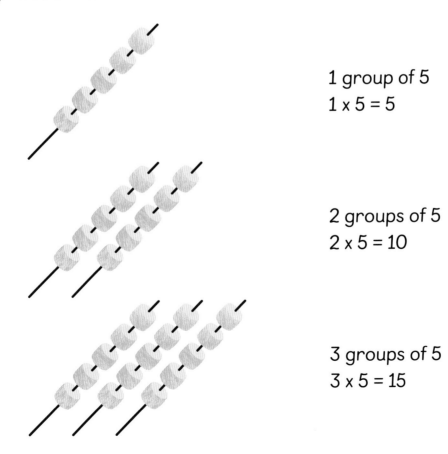

1 group of 5
1 x 5 = 5

2 groups of 5
2 x 5 = 10

3 groups of 5
3 x 5 = 15

There are 15 marshmallows altogether.

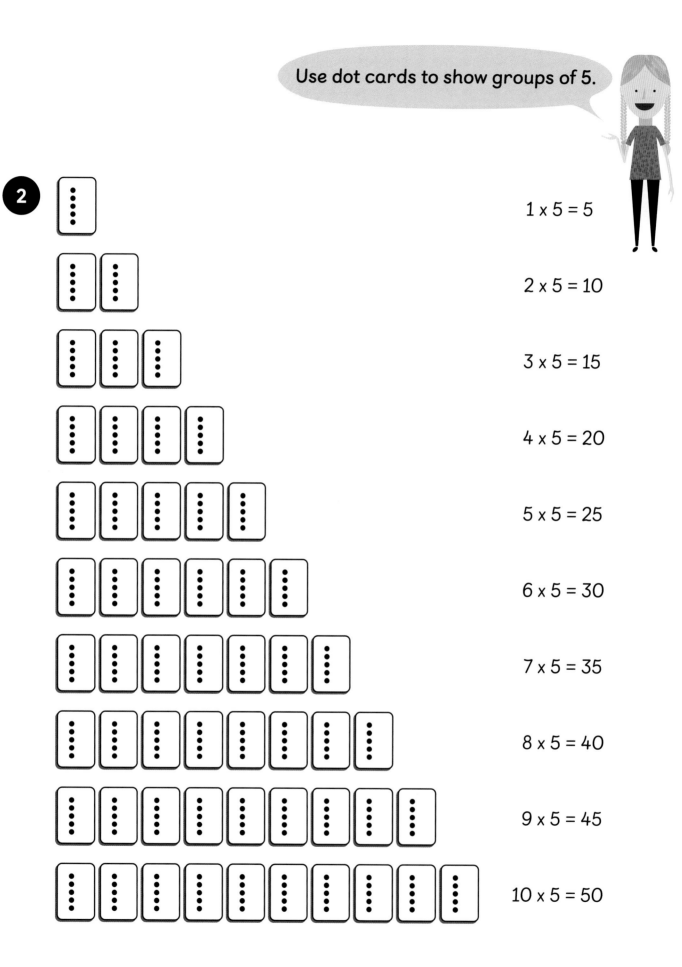

2

1 x 5 = 5

2 x 5 = 10

3 x 5 = 15

4 x 5 = 20

5 x 5 = 25

6 x 5 = 30

7 x 5 = 35

8 x 5 = 40

9 x 5 = 45

10 x 5 = 50

Guided Practice

1 Complete the multiplication equation.

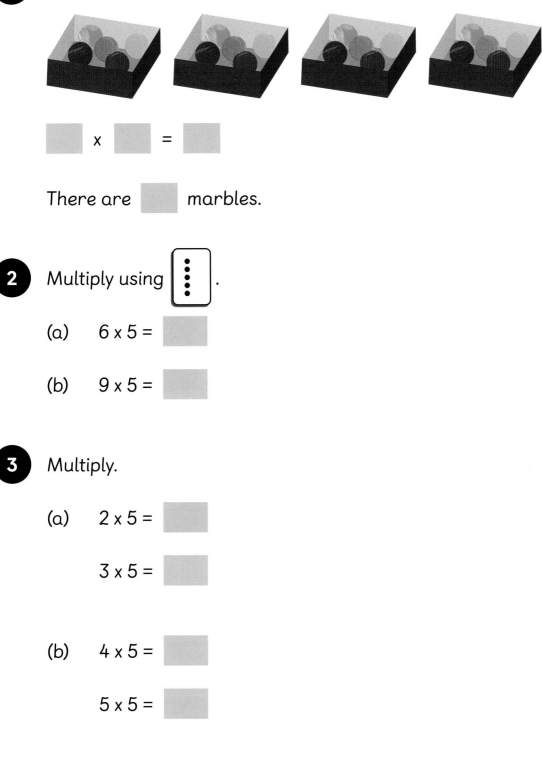

[ ] x [ ] = [ ]

There are [ ] marbles.

2 Multiply using ⠿.

(a) 6 x 5 = [ ]

(b) 9 x 5 = [ ]

3 Multiply.

(a) 2 x 5 = [ ]

     3 x 5 = [ ]

(b) 4 x 5 = [ ]

     5 x 5 = [ ]

Complete Worksheet **4** · Page **85 – 88**

5 Times Table

In Focus

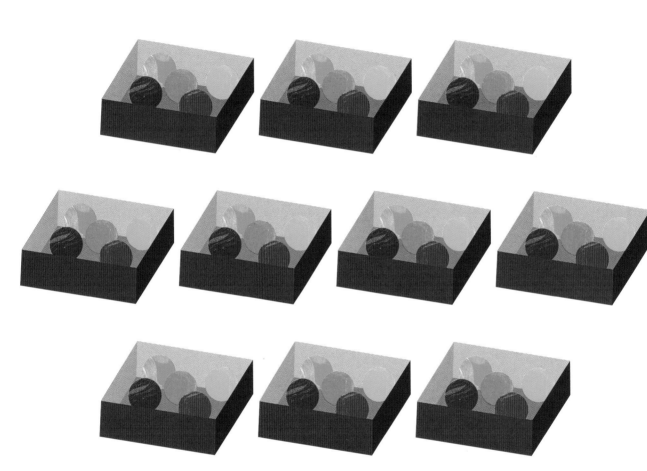

Charles has 10 boxes of marbles.
Each box has 5 marbles.
How many marbles does he have in all?

1 Count in fives.

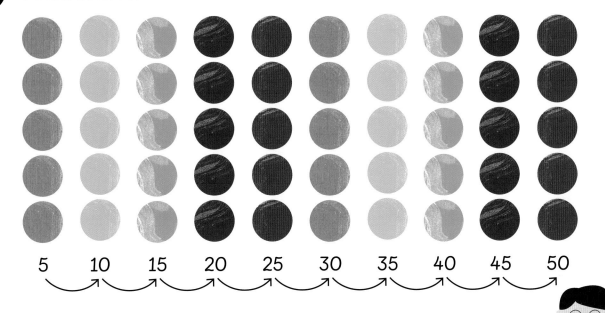

5   10   15   20   25   30   35   40   45   50

He has 50 marbles in all.

5, 10, 15, 20, 25, 30, 35, 40, 45, 50

1	2	3	4	5	6	7	8	9	10
11	12	13	14	15	16	17	18	19	20
21	22	23	24	25	26	27	28	29	30
31	32	33	34	35	36	37	38	39	40
41	42	43	44	45	46	47	48	49	50

What number pattern do you see on the number chart?

2   9 x 5 = [   ]

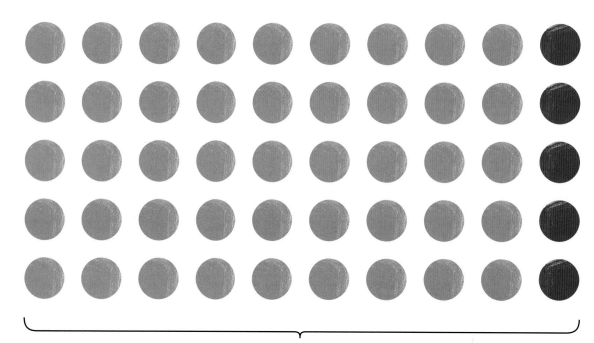

10 x 5 = 50

9 x 5 = 50 − 5

       = 45

10 x 5 = 50
9 x 5 is 5 less than 50.

1 Multiply using .

(a) 8 x 5 =

7 x 5 =

(b) 10 x 5 =

9 x 5 =

2 Complete the multiplication table.

1 x 5 =

2 x 5 =

3 x 5 =

4 x 5 =

5 x 5 =

6 x 5 =

7 x 5 =

8 x 5 =

9 x 5 =

10 x 5 =

Use 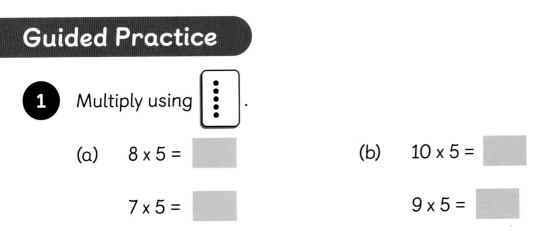 if necessary.

Complete Worksheet **5** • Page **89 – 90**

10 Times Table

In Focus

How many children are there?

Let's Learn

1 1 group has 10 children.

1 group of 10
$1 \times 10 = 10$

2 groups of 10
$2 \times 10 = 20$

There are 20 children.

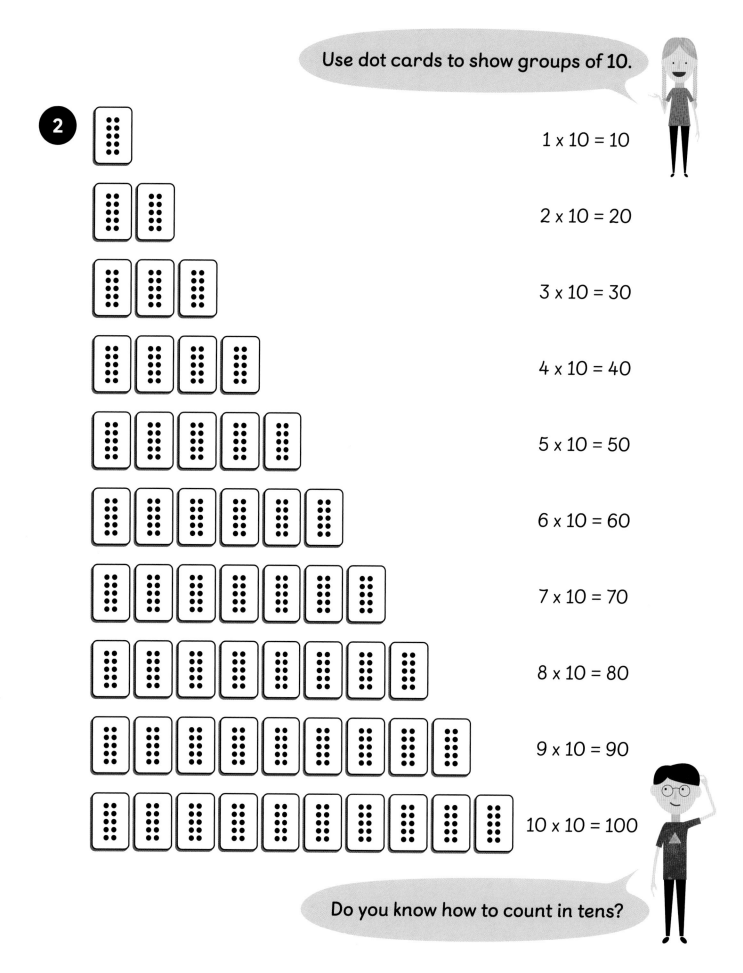

Use dot cards to show groups of 10.

2

1 x 10 = 10

2 x 10 = 20

3 x 10 = 30

4 x 10 = 40

5 x 10 = 50

6 x 10 = 60

7 x 10 = 70

8 x 10 = 80

9 x 10 = 90

10 x 10 = 100

Do you know how to count in tens?

1 Complete the multiplication equation.

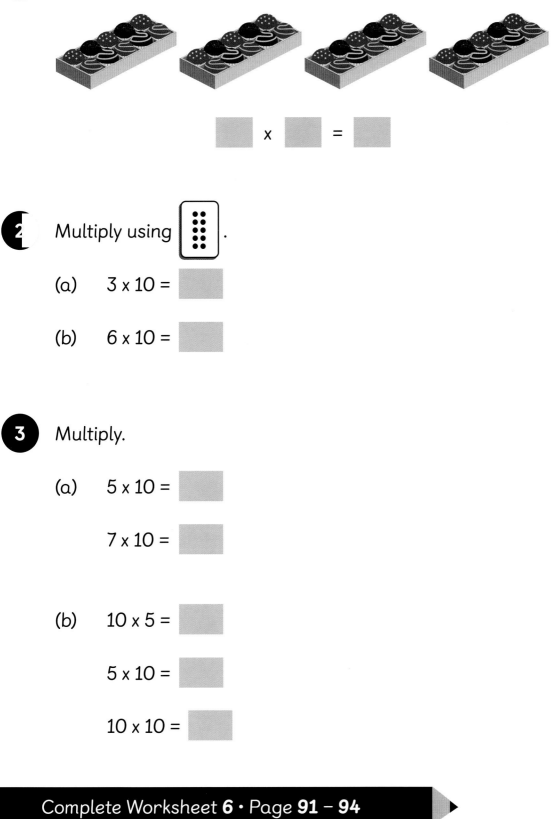

☐ x ☐ = ☐

2 Multiply using ⚅⚅ .

(a)   3 x 10 = ☐

(b)   6 x 10 = ☐

3 Multiply.

(a)   5 x 10 = ☐

   7 x 10 = ☐

(b)   10 x 5 = ☐

   5 x 10 = ☐

   10 x 10 = ☐

Complete Worksheet 6 · Page 91 – 94

10 Times Table

In Focus

How many flowers are there?

Let's Learn

5 groups of 10
5 × 10

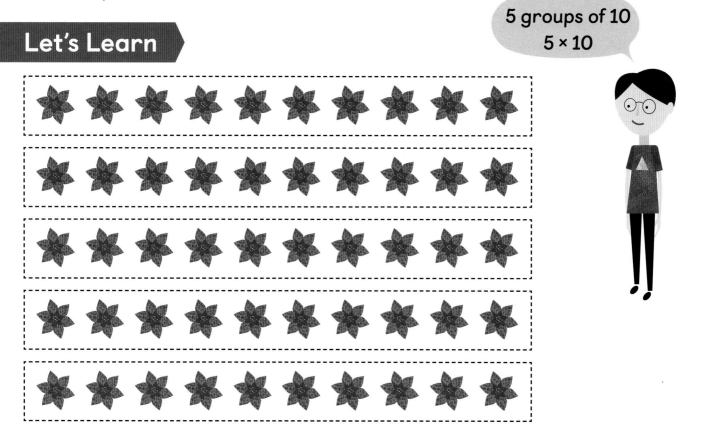

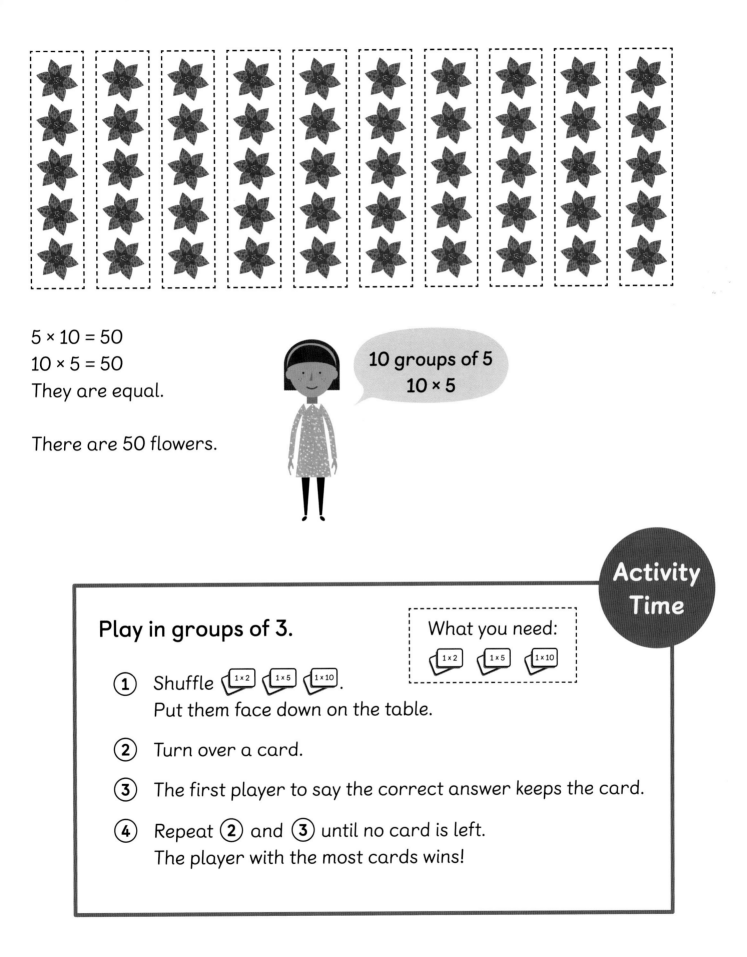

$5 \times 10 = 50$
$10 \times 5 = 50$
They are equal.

There are 50 flowers.

10 groups of 5
10×5

Play in groups of 3.

What you need:
1 × 2   1 × 5   1 × 10

① Shuffle 1 × 2   1 × 5   1 × 10 .
   Put them face down on the table.

② Turn over a card.

③ The first player to say the correct answer keeps the card.

④ Repeat ② and ③ until no card is left.
   The player with the most cards wins!

Guided Practice

1 Complete the multiplication table.

1 x 10 =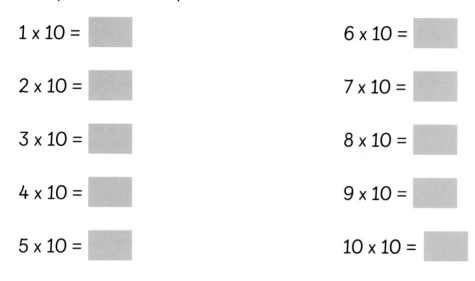

2 x 10 =

3 x 10 =

4 x 10 =

5 x 10 =

6 x 10 =

7 x 10 =

8 x 10 =

9 x 10 =

10 x 10 =

2 Multiply.

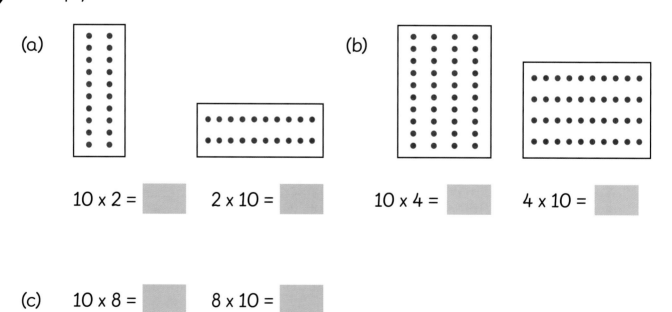

(a)

10 x 2 =   2 x 10 =

(b)

10 x 4 =   4 x 10 =

(c)   10 x 8 =   8 x 10 =

Complete Worksheet 7 · Page 95 – 97

Multiplying by 2, 5 and 10

In Focus

5 × 2 = 10

2 × 5 = 10

Who is correct?
Why?

Let's Learn

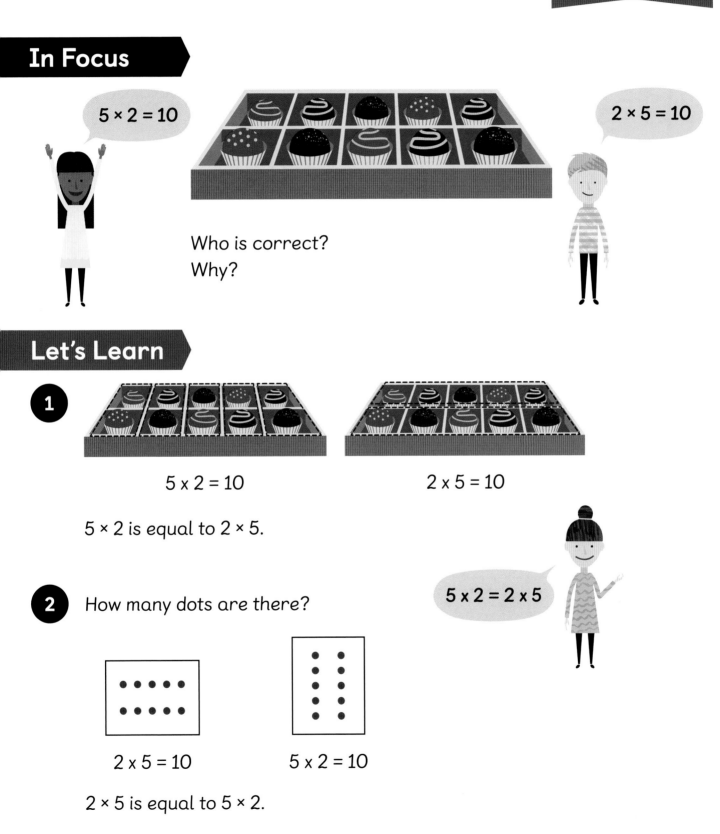

1

5 x 2 = 10

2 x 5 = 10

5 × 2 is equal to 2 × 5.

5 × 2 = 2 × 5

2 How many dots are there?

2 x 5 = 10

5 x 2 = 10

2 × 5 is equal to 5 × 2.

1 Multiply using the dot diagrams.

(a)

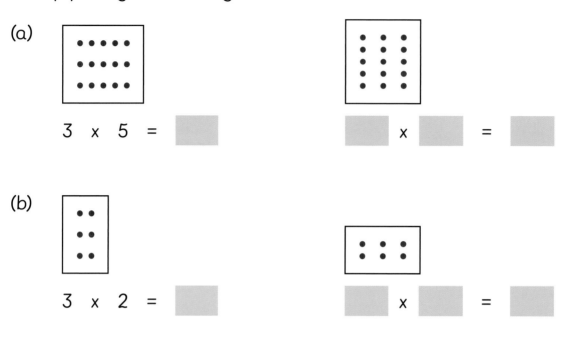

3 x 5 = ▢

▢ x ▢ = ▢

(b)

3 x 2 = ▢

▢ x ▢ = ▢

2 Multiply.

(a) 4 x 5 = ▢

5 x 4 = ▢

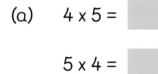

(b) 8 x 2 = ▢

2 x 8 = ▢

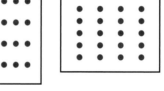

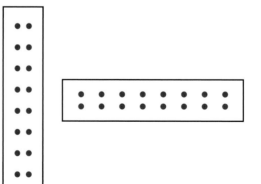

Complete Worksheet **8** · Page **98 – 101**

Multiplying by 2, 5 and 10

In Focus

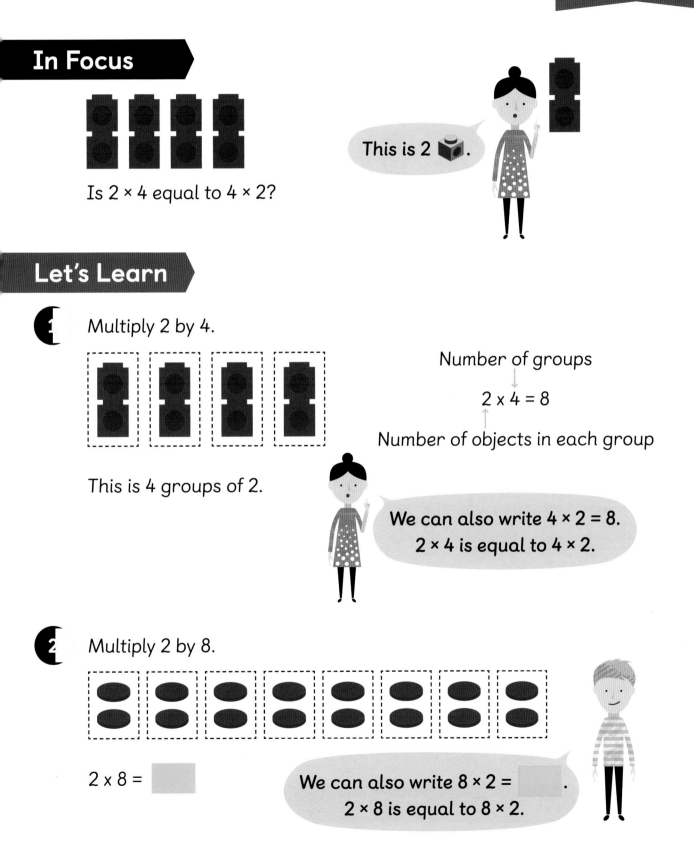

Is 2 × 4 equal to 4 × 2?

This is 2 🎲.

Let's Learn

1 Multiply 2 by 4.

This is 4 groups of 2.

Number of groups
↓
2 × 4 = 8
↑
Number of objects in each group

We can also write 4 × 2 = 8.
2 × 4 is equal to 4 × 2.

2 Multiply 2 by 8.

2 × 8 = ▢

We can also write 8 × 2 = ▢ .
2 × 8 is equal to 8 × 2.

3 Multiply 3 by 5.

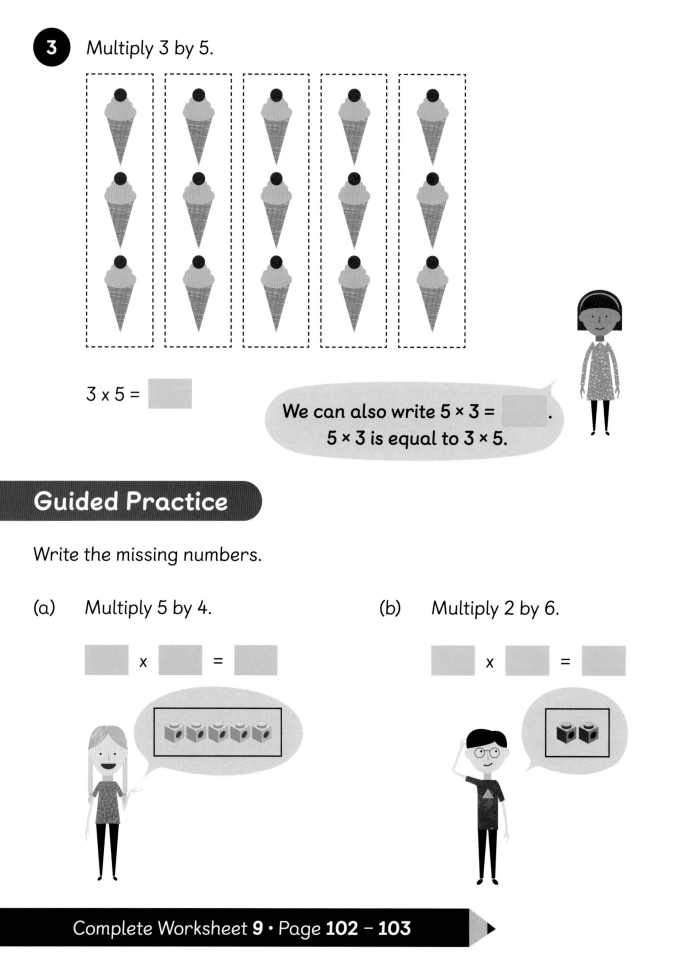

$3 \times 5 = $ ▢

We can also write $5 \times 3 = $ ▢.
5×3 is equal to 3×5.

Guided Practice

Write the missing numbers.

(a) Multiply 5 by 4.

▢ x ▢ = ▢

(b) Multiply 2 by 6.

▢ x ▢ = ▢

Complete Worksheet **9** • Page **102 – 103**

Solving Word Problems

In Focus

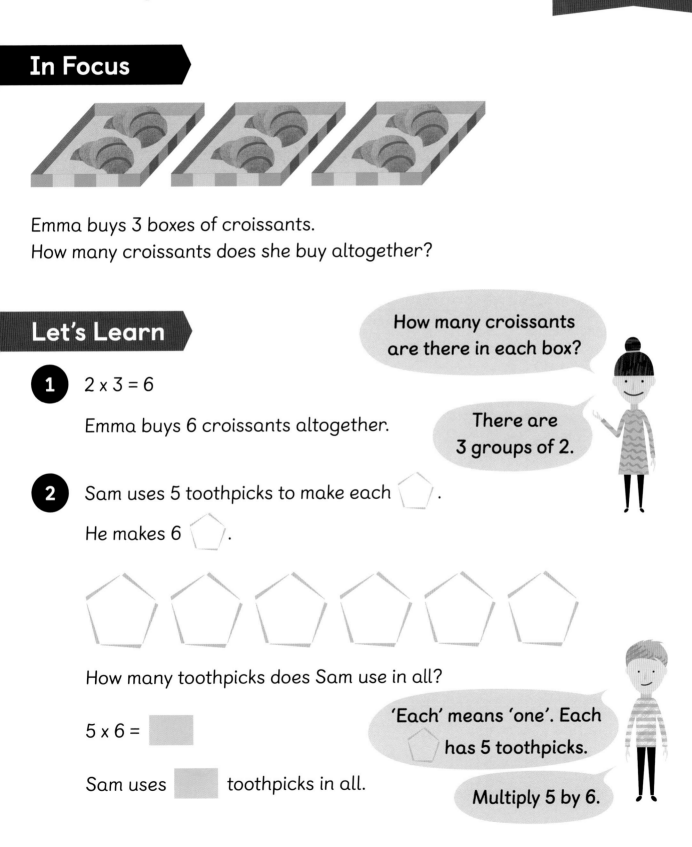

Emma buys 3 boxes of croissants.
How many croissants does she buy altogether?

Let's Learn

1 2 x 3 = 6

Emma buys 6 croissants altogether.

> How many croissants are there in each box?

> There are 3 groups of 2.

2 Sam uses 5 toothpicks to make each ⬠ .

He makes 6 ⬠ .

How many toothpicks does Sam use in all?

5 x 6 = ▢

Sam uses ▢ toothpicks in all.

> 'Each' means 'one'. Each ⬠ has 5 toothpicks.

> Multiply 5 by 6.

Work in groups of 4.

Make three multiplication stories.
Draw pictures to show your stories.

What you need:

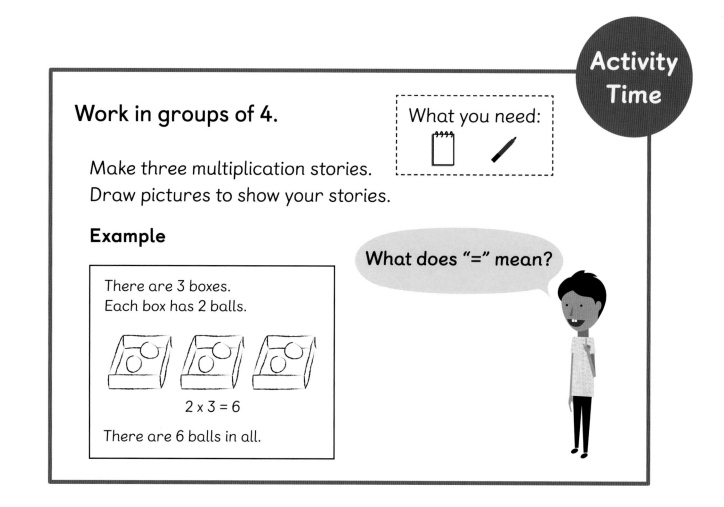

Example

There are 3 boxes.
Each box has 2 balls.

2 x 3 = 6

There are 6 balls in all.

What does "=" mean?

Guided Practice

1 Each bag holds 5 apples.
How many apples are there in 3 bags?

2 Amira has 7 pies.
She cuts each pie into 10 slices.
How many slices of pie are there in all?

3 A bicycle has 2 wheels.
How many wheels do 4 bicycles have?

Complete Worksheet 10 · Page 104 – 108

Holly wants to arrange 20 cards for a memory game.
Each row should have the same number of cards.
This is one way she can arrange the cards.

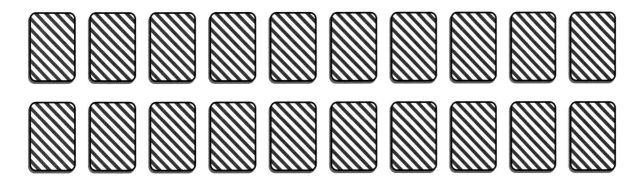

2 rows of 10

Draw another way that she can arrange the cards.
You may use ▨ to help you.

Maths Journal

Complete the two problems.
Work with your classmates to solve each problem.

1 _____ has _____ packets.
    (name)   (number from 1 to 10)

   Each packet has 5 _____.
                        (objects)

   How many _____ does _____ have altogether?
              (objects)   (name)

2 [   ] gives 10 [   ] to each of her children.
(name)   (objects)

She has [   ] children.
(number from 1 to 10)

How many [   ] does [   ] have altogether?
(objects)   (name)

I know how to...

☐ do my 2 times table.

☐ do my 5 times table.

☐ do my 10 times table.

☐ write multiplication equations.

☐ solve word problems using the 2, 5 and 10 times tables.

Self Check

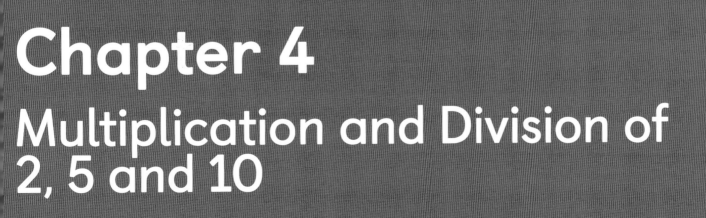

How many bags of chocolate can Emma get?

Chapter 4
Multiplication and Division of 2, 5 and 10

Grouping

In Focus

How many bags of chocolate can Emma get?

Divide 20 by 2 to find the number of groups. There are 10 groups of 2.

÷ means to divide. 20 ÷ 2 is equal to 10.

Let's Learn

There are 20 chocolates.

Put 2 chocolates in each bag.

Emma gets 10 bags of chocolate.

20 ÷ 2 = 10 is a **division equation**.

20 ÷ 2 = 10 is read as twenty **divided by** two **equals** ten.

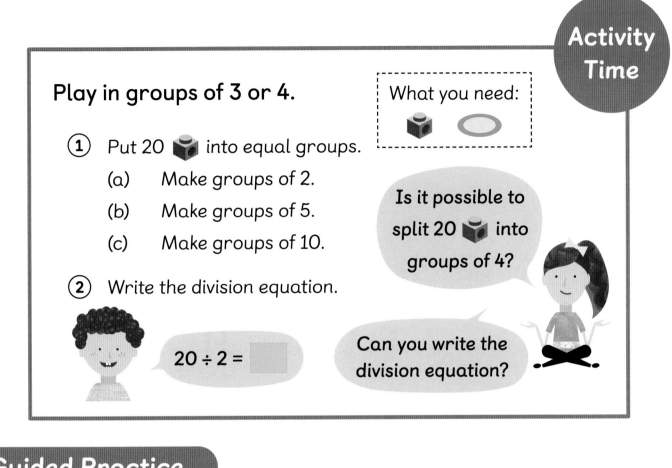

Play in groups of 3 or 4.

What you need:

① Put 20 🎲 into equal groups.

(a)   Make groups of 2.

(b)   Make groups of 5.

(c)   Make groups of 10.

② Write the division equation.

20 ÷ 2 = ▢

Is it possible to split 20 🎲 into groups of 4?

Can you write the division equation?

Guided Practice

1 Circle to show groups of 2.
How many groups are there?

▢ ÷ ▢ = ▢

There are ▢ groups.

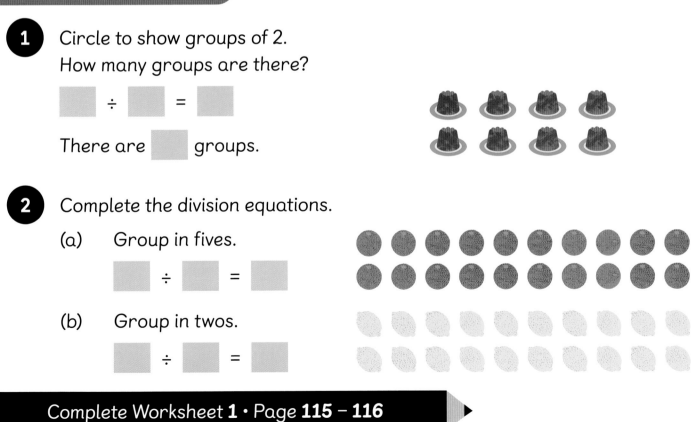

2 Complete the division equations.

(a)   Group in fives.

▢ ÷ ▢ = ▢

(b)   Group in twos.

▢ ÷ ▢ = ▢

Complete Worksheet 1 · Page 115 – 116

Sharing

In Focus

How can the sausages be put equally on 2 plates?
What is the number of sausages on each plate?

Let's Learn

There are 18 sausages.

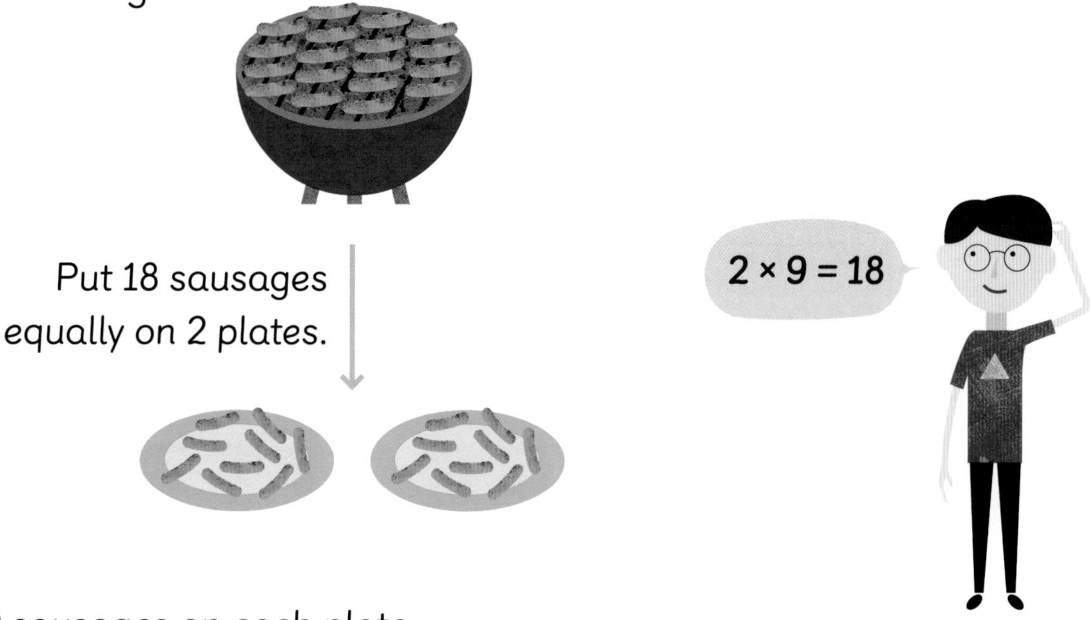

Put 18 sausages
equally on 2 plates.

$2 \times 9 = 18$

There are 9 sausages on each plate.

$18 \div 2 = 9$

Play in pairs.

What you need:
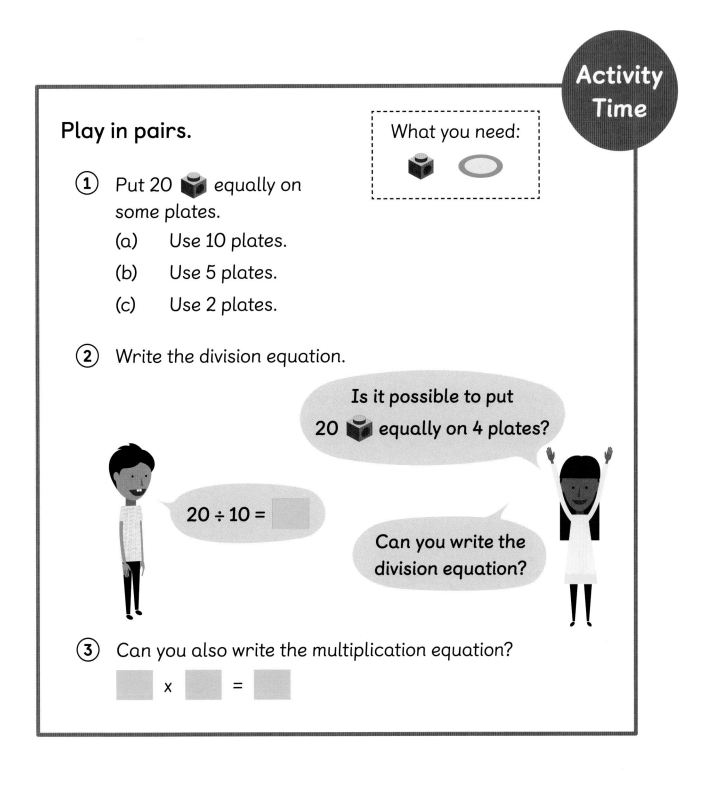

① Put 20 🎲 equally on some plates.

    (a)   Use 10 plates.

    (b)   Use 5 plates.

    (c)   Use 2 plates.

② Write the division equation.

Is it possible to put 20 🎲 equally on 4 plates?

$20 \div 10 =$ ▢

Can you write the division equation?

③ Can you also write the multiplication equation?

▢ × ▢ = ▢

Guided Practice

1 Ruby has 10 fish.
She puts them equally into 5 bowls.

☐ x 5 = 10

☐ ÷ ☐ = ☐

There are ☐ fish in each bowl.

2 Write the missing numbers.

(a) Put 16 apples equally in 2 baskets.

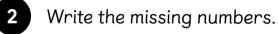

☐ ÷ ☐ = ☐

2 x ☐ = ☐

(b) Put 15 oranges equally on 5 plates.

☐ ÷ ☐ = ☐

5 x ☐ = ☐

Complete Worksheet 2 · Page 117 – 118

Dividing by 2

In Focus

Amira packs 8 bread rolls in some baskets.
Each basket has 2 bread rolls.
How many baskets does Amira need?

Let's Learn

There are 8 bread rolls.

Use to stand for bread rolls and ⬭ to stand for baskets.

$4 \times 2 = 8$
$8 \div 2 = 4$

Put 2 bread rolls in each basket.

$8 \div 2 = 4$

Amira needs 4 baskets.

What if Amira packs the 8 bread rolls equally in 2 baskets?

Guided Practice

1 Write the missing numbers.

(a)

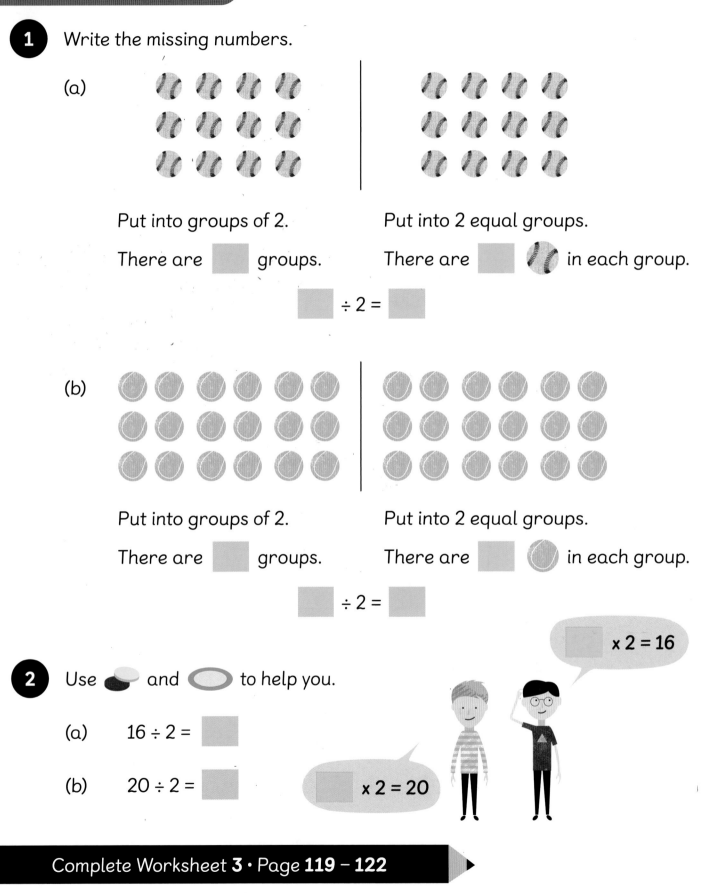

Put into groups of 2.

There are ☐ groups.

Put into 2 equal groups.

There are ☐ 🏐 in each group.

☐ ÷ 2 = ☐

(b)

Put into groups of 2.

There are ☐ groups.

Put into 2 equal groups.

There are ☐ ⚪ in each group.

☐ ÷ 2 = ☐

☐ x 2 = 16

2 Use ⬤ and ⬭ to help you.

(a) 16 ÷ 2 = ☐

(b) 20 ÷ 2 = ☐

☐ x 2 = 20

Complete Worksheet **3** · Page **119 – 122**

Dividing by 5

In Focus

Ravi puts 5 cookies on each tray.
How many trays of cookies are there?

Let's Learn

There are 15 cookies.

Use ⬤ to stand for cookies and ▱ to stand for the trays.

$3 × 5 = 15$
$15 ÷ 5 = 3$

Put 5 cookies on each tray.

$15 ÷ 5 = 3$

There are 3 trays of cookies.

What if Ravi puts the 15 cookies equally on 5 trays?

1 Write the missing numbers.

(a)

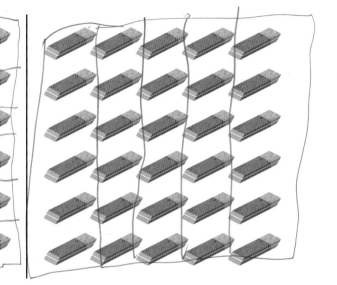

Put into groups of 5.

There are 6 ① groups.

Put into 5 equal groups.

There are 6 ①  in each group.

$30 \div 5 = 6$ ①

(b)

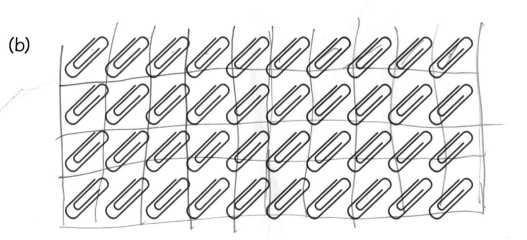

Put into groups of 5.

There are 8 ① groups.

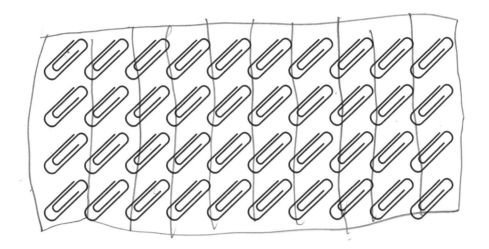

Put into 5 equal groups.

There are 4 🖇 in each group.

4̶0̶ ÷ 5 = 8

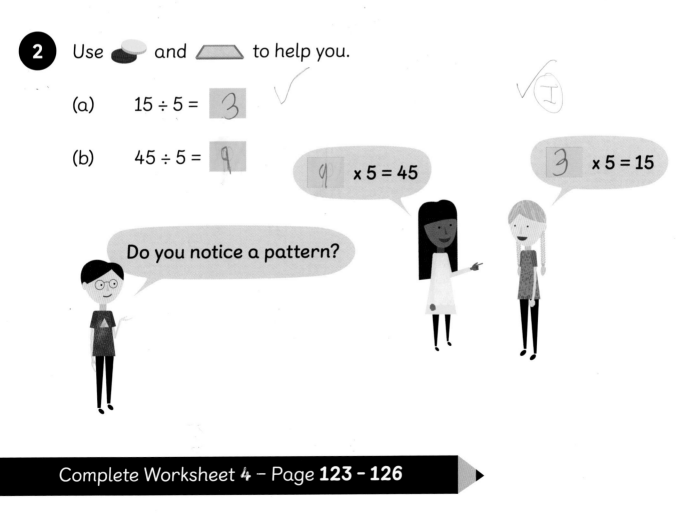

2 Use 🪙 and ▱ to help you.

(a) 15 ÷ 5 = 3 ✓

(b) 45 ÷ 5 = 9

9 x 5 = 45

3 x 5 = 15

Do you notice a pattern?

Complete Worksheet 4 – Page **123 – 126**

Dividing by 10

In Focus

60 sweets are packed into jars.
Each jar contains 10 sweets.
How many jars of sweets are there?

There are 60 sweets.

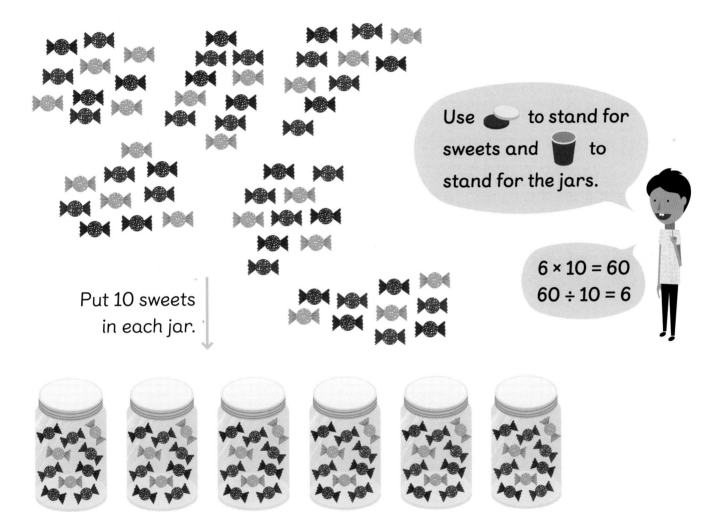

Use 🔘 to stand for sweets and 🥤 to stand for the jars.

$6 \times 10 = 60$
$60 \div 10 = 6$

Put 10 sweets in each jar.

$60 \div 10 = 6$

There are 6 jars of sweets.

What if the 60 sweets are packed equally into 10 jars?

Play in pairs.

What you need:

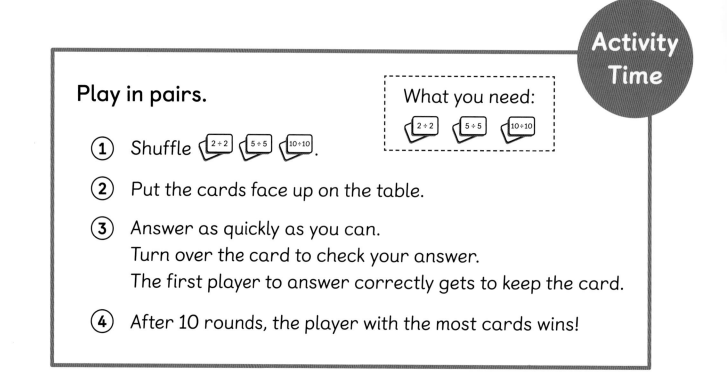

① Shuffle [2÷2] [5÷5] [10÷10].

② Put the cards face up on the table.

③ Answer as quickly as you can.
Turn over the card to check your answer.
The first player to answer correctly gets to keep the card.

④ After 10 rounds, the player with the most cards wins!

Guided Practice

 Write the missing numbers.

Put into groups of 10.

There are ▢ groups.

Put into 10 equal groups.

There are ▢ 🌰 in each group.

▢ ÷ 10 = ▢

2 Use 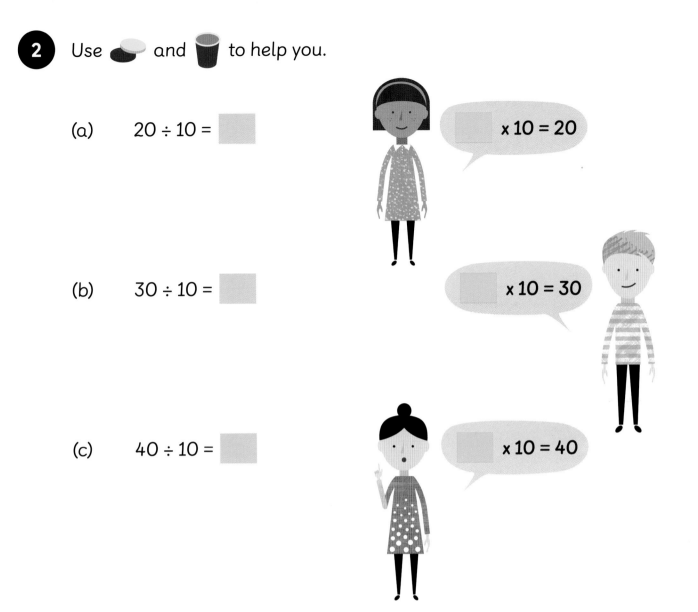 and to help you.

(a) $20 \div 10 = $ [ ]

[ ] x 10 = 20

(b) $30 \div 10 = $ [ ]

[ ] x 10 = 30

(c) $40 \div 10 = $ [ ]

[ ] x 10 = 40

Complete Worksheet **5** – Page **127 - 130**

Multiplication and Division

In Focus

How can we put the buns in equal groups?

Let's Learn

1 Put 10 buns in groups of 2.
How many plates are there?

10 ÷ 2 = 5

There are 5 plates.

There are 5 plates.
There are 2 buns on each plate.
5 × 2 = 10

Put 10 buns equally on 5 plates.
How many buns are there on each plate?

$10 \div 2 = 5$

There are 2 buns on each plate.

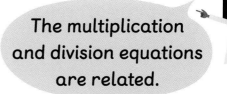

There are 2 buns
on each plate.
There are 5 plates.
$2 \times 5 = 10$

We can make a family of multiplication and division facts.

$5 \times 2 = 10$ ——————— $10 \div 2 = 5$
$2 \times 5 = 10$ ——————— $10 \div 5 = 2$

The multiplication
and division equations
are related.

 2 Look at the picture.
Make a family of multiplication and division facts.

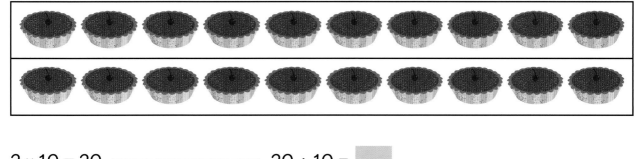

$2 \times 10 = 20$ ——————— $20 \div 10 = $ ▢

$10 \times 2 = 20$ ——————— $20 \div 2 = $ ▢

Work in pairs.

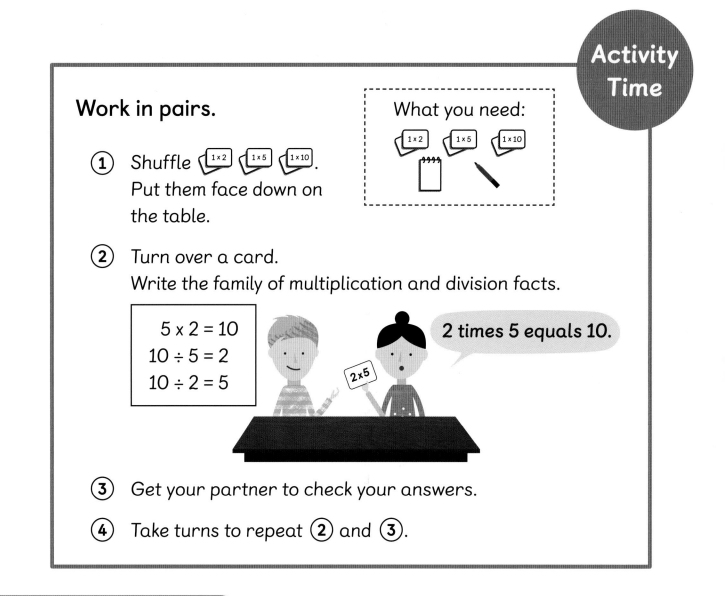

What you need:

1. Shuffle 1×2 1×5 1×10.
   Put them face down on the table.

2. Turn over a card.
   Write the family of multiplication and division facts.

   $5 \times 2 = 10$
   $10 \div 5 = 2$
   $10 \div 2 = 5$

   2 times 5 equals 10.

3. Get your partner to check your answers.

4. Take turns to repeat ② and ③.

Guided Practice

Make a family of multiplication and division facts.

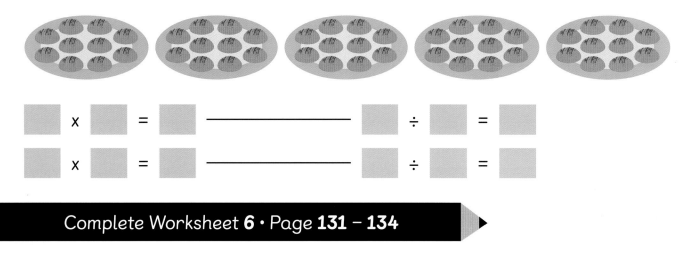

☐ x ☐ = ☐ ——————— ☐ ÷ ☐ = ☐

☐ x ☐ = ☐ ——————— ☐ ÷ ☐ = ☐

Complete Worksheet 6 · Page 131 – 134

Solving Word Problems

In Focus

How can Amira share 12 key chains equally between 2 children?

Let's Learn

Amira has 12 key chains.
She shares the key chains equally between 2 children.
How many key chains does each child get?

Method 1   Use 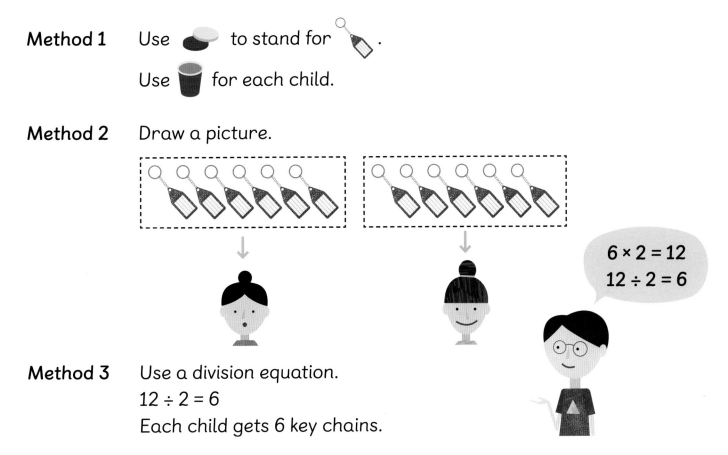 to stand for .

Use for each child.

Method 2   Draw a picture.

$6 \times 2 = 12$
$12 \div 2 = 6$

Method 3   Use a division equation.
$12 \div 2 = 6$
Each child gets 6 key chains.

1 Ruby has 15 marshmallows.
She packs 5 marshmallows into each bag.
How many bags does Ruby need?

[ ] x 5 = 15

Method 1   Use ⬤ to stand for 🔘 .

Use 🥤 for each bag.

Method 2   Draw a picture.

Method 3   Use a division equation.

[ ] ÷ [ ] = [ ]

Ruby needs  bags.

2 Hannah has 50 paper clips.
She gives some children 10 paper clips each.
How many children does Hannah give the paper clips to?

Method 1   Use 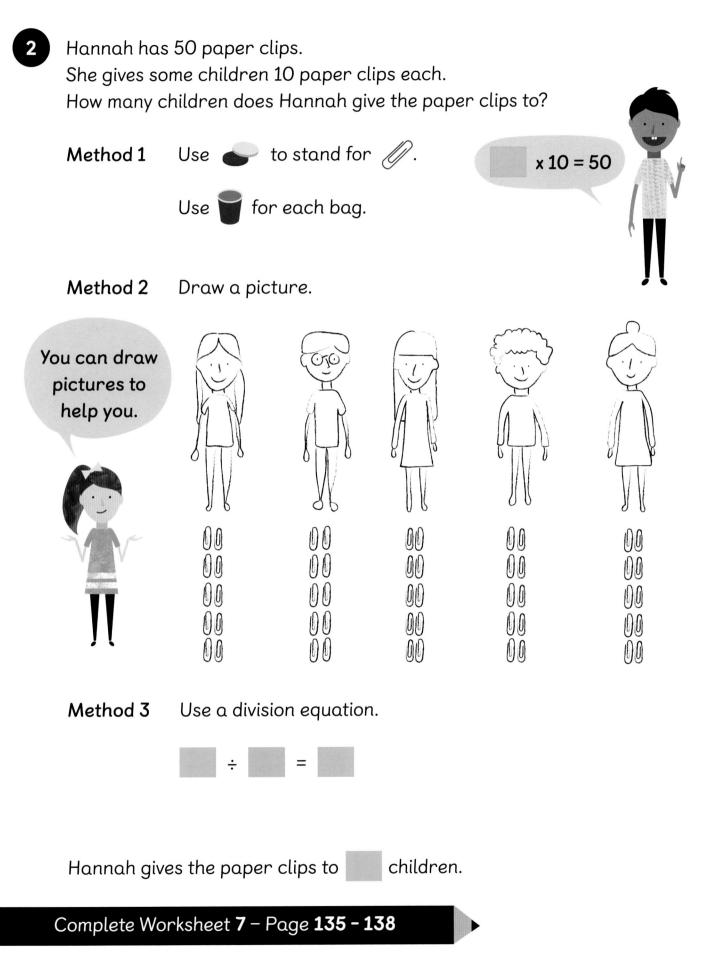 to stand for ✏.

Use ▮ for each bag.

[ ] x 10 = 50

Method 2   Draw a picture.

You can draw pictures to help you.

Method 3   Use a division equation.

[ ] ÷ [ ] = [ ]

Hannah gives the paper clips to [ ] children.

Complete Worksheet **7** – Page **135 – 138** ▶

Odd and Even Numbers

In Focus

Compare the boxes of chocolate cupcakes and the boxes of strawberry cupcakes. What do you notice?

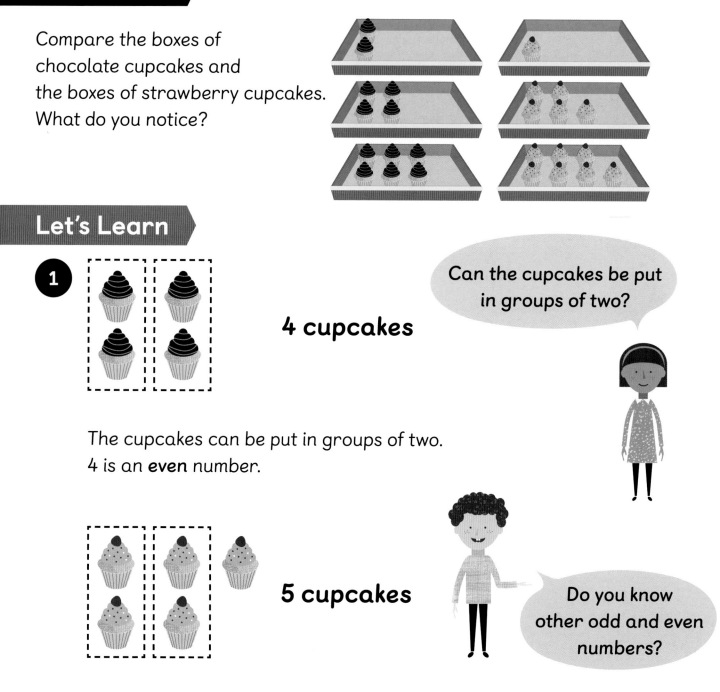

Let's Learn

1 4 cupcakes

Can the cupcakes be put in groups of two?

The cupcakes can be put in groups of two.
4 is an **even** number.

5 cupcakes

Do you know other odd and even numbers?

The strawberry cupcakes cannot be put in groups of two.
5 is an **odd** number.

2

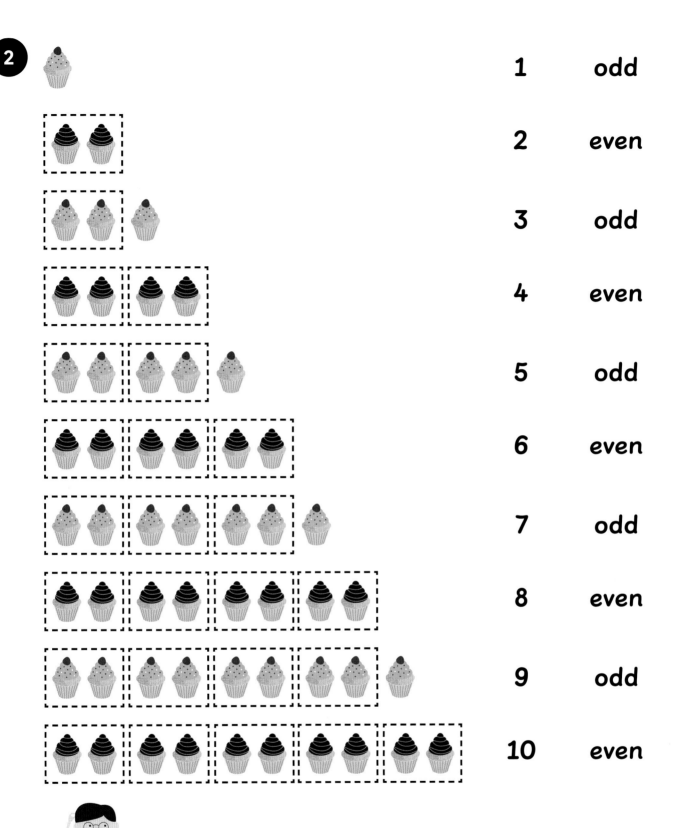

1	odd
2	even
3	odd
4	even
5	odd
6	even
7	odd
8	even
9	odd
10	even

What do you notice about even and odd numbers?

3 How do you find out if 12 is an odd or even number?

12

$12 \div 2 = 6$

12 is in the 2 times table. It is an even number.

We can divide the number by 2.

$6 \times 2 = 12$

4

| 12 | 13 | 14 | 15 | 16 | 17 |

▨ , ▨ and ▨ are odd numbers.

▨ , ▨ and ▨ are even numbers.

Can you explain your answers?

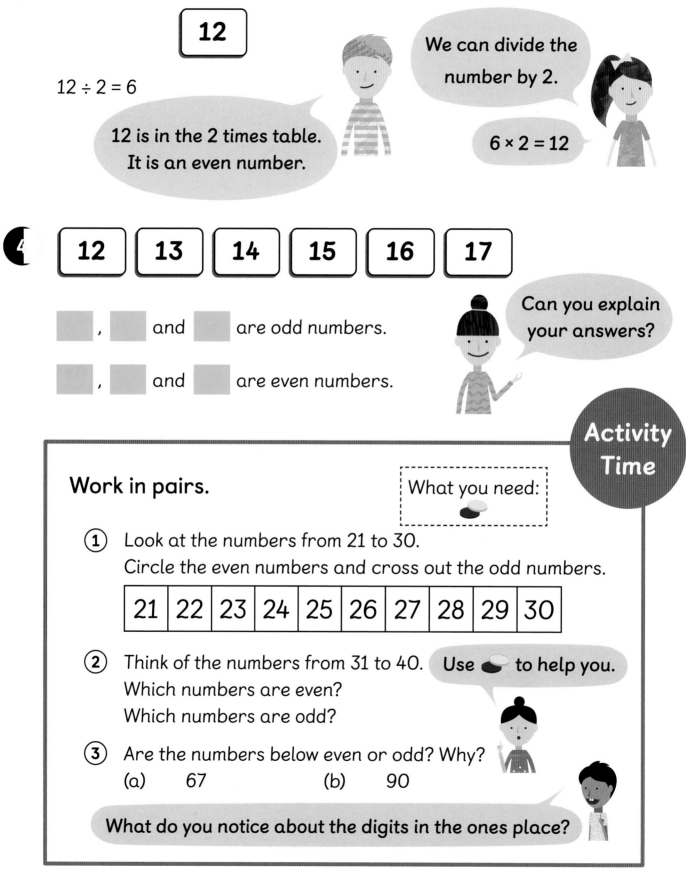

Activity Time

Work in pairs.

What you need:

① Look at the numbers from 21 to 30.
Circle the even numbers and cross out the odd numbers.

| 21 | 22 | 23 | 24 | 25 | 26 | 27 | 28 | 29 | 30 |

② Think of the numbers from 31 to 40. Use ⬤ to help you.
Which numbers are even?
Which numbers are odd?

③ Are the numbers below even or odd? Why?
   (a)   67   (b)   90

What do you notice about the digits in the ones place?

1   Look at the numbers given.
    Which are even numbers? Which are odd numbers?

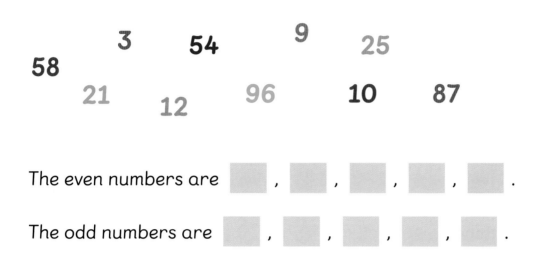

The even numbers are ⬜ , ⬜ , ⬜ , ⬜ , ⬜ .

The odd numbers are ⬜ , ⬜ , ⬜ , ⬜ , ⬜ .

2   Look at the digits.

(a)   Form the greatest 2-digit even number.   ⬜

(b)   Form the smallest 2-digit odd number.   ⬜

Complete Worksheet 8 • Page 139 – 141

Look at the picture.

How many marbles should Emma give to Charles so that they have the same number of marbles?

Emma should give Charles ☐ marbles.

Use ● to help you. How many marbles do they have altogether?

Maths Journal

Look at the sentence.

Write a division equation and make a division story.

Use 🧊 to help you divide.

Divide 35 by 5

Self Check

I know how to...

☐ divide a number by 2.

☐ divide a number by 5.

☐ divide a number by 10.

☐ write multiplication and division equations.

☐ write a family of multiplication and division facts.

☐ solve word problems involving multiplication and division.

☐ recognise odd and even numbers.

How long is my bed?

Chapter 5
Length

Measuring Length in Metres

In Focus

We have learnt that we can use different objects to measure length.
Use 1 stick ▬▬▬ as 1 unit.

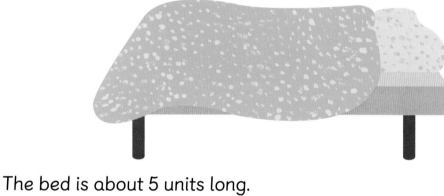

The bed is about 5 units long.
What other measurements can we use?

> Your teacher will show you an actual tape measure.

Let's Learn

1 ┃▬▬▬▬▬▬▬▬▬▬▬▬▬▬┃
◄─────────── 1 metre ───────────►

This is a tape measure.
It is one **metre** long.
A metre is a unit of length.
We write **m** for metre.

> We read **1 m** as **one metre**.

2 We can measure in metres.

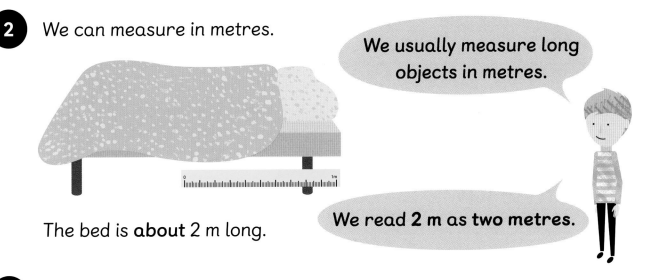

We usually measure long objects in metres.

We read **2 m** as **two metres.**

The bed is **about** 2 m long.

3 We can measure the length of objects around us.

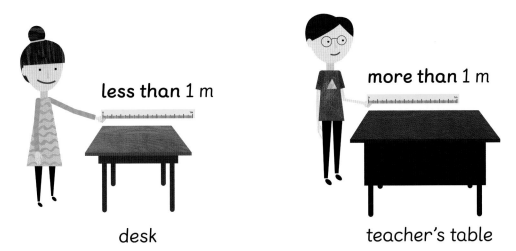

less than 1 m

desk

more than 1 m

teacher's table

The length of the desk is **shorter than** 1 m.
The length of the teacher's table is **longer than** 1 m.

Show 1 m using your arm span.

The height of the cupboard is about 2 m.

Work in groups of 2 to 4.

① Measure your arm span with a 🗒️ .
Is it longer or shorter than 1 m?

② Measure the length, width and height of some of the things around us.
Are they more than 1 m, about 1 m or less than 1 m?

Use the 🗒️ to check.

object	my guess	check
length of whiteboard	more than 1 m	more than 1 m
width of classroom window		
height of teacher's table		
height of my chair		
length of my friend's arm span		
length of my waistline		

What is the length of my waistline?

What is the length of Charles' arm span?

③ Tell your classmates what your group finds.

Complete Worksheet 1 · Page 155 – 158

Measuring Length in Centimetres

In Focus

What is the length of the ruler?

Let's Learn

1   1 cm

This is a centimetre ruler.
The **centimetre** is a smaller unit of length.
We write **cm** for centimetre.

The centimetre ruler is 15 cm long.

When do we measure objects in centimetres? Why?

We read **15 cm** as fifteen centimetres.

2 How long is the pencil?

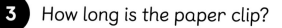

The length of the pencil is about 12 cm.

> Place the pencil at the zero mark.
> Look at the marking at the other end.

3 How long is the paper clip?

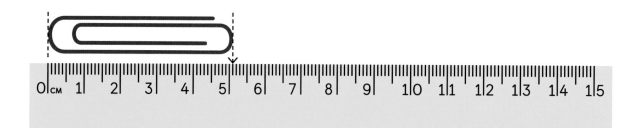

The length of the paper clip is about [ ] cm.

4 What is the height of the carton of milk?

The height of the carton of milk is about ⬜ cm.

5 How long is the colouring pen?

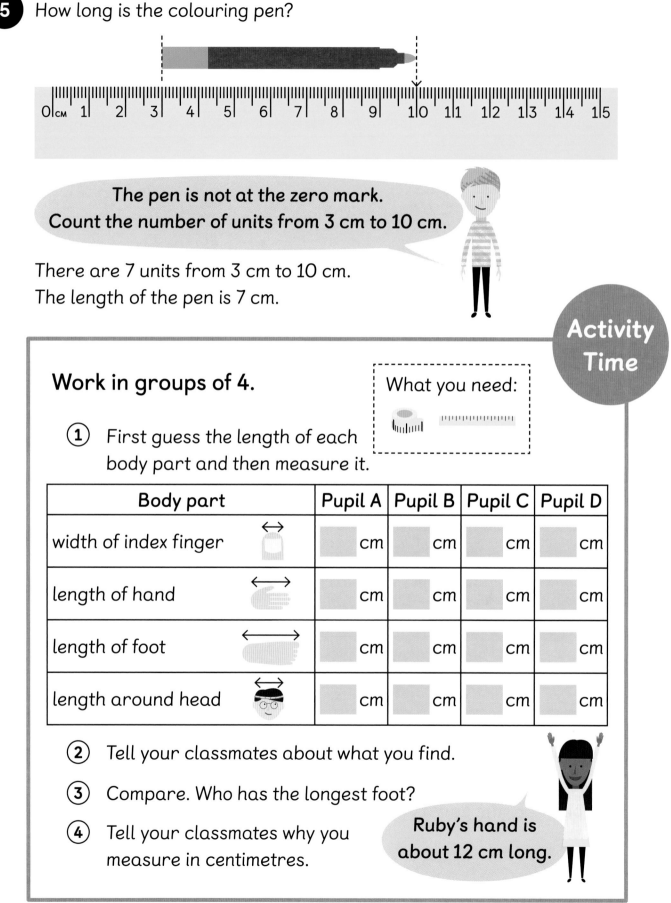

The pen is not at the zero mark.
Count the number of units from 3 cm to 10 cm.

There are 7 units from 3 cm to 10 cm.
The length of the pen is 7 cm.

Activity Time

Work in groups of 4.

What you need:

① First guess the length of each body part and then measure it.

Body part		Pupil A	Pupil B	Pupil C	Pupil D
width of index finger		cm	cm	cm	cm
length of hand		cm	cm	cm	cm
length of foot		cm	cm	cm	cm
length around head		cm	cm	cm	cm

② Tell your classmates about what you find.

③ Compare. Who has the longest foot?

④ Tell your classmates why you measure in centimetres.

Ruby's hand is about 12 cm long.

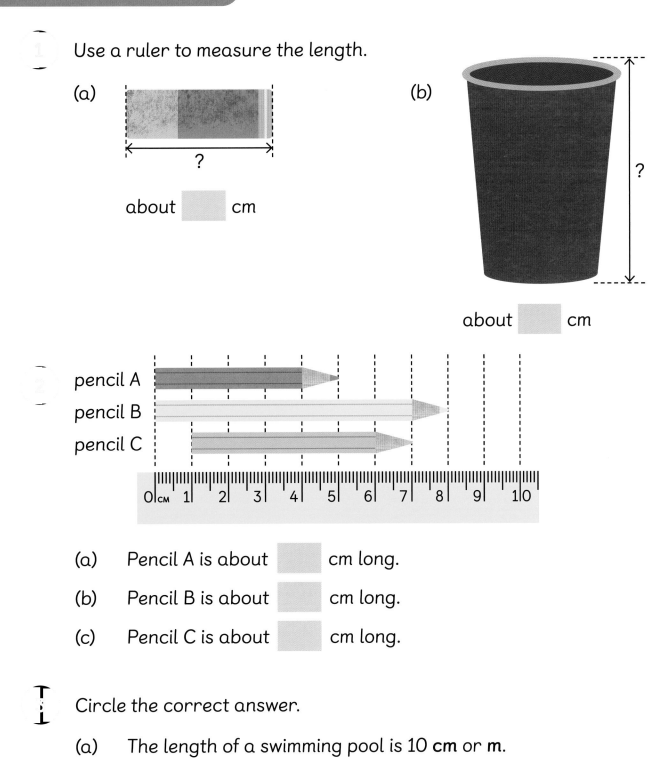

1. Use a ruler to measure the length.

(a)

?

about _____ cm

(b)

?

about _____ cm

2.

pencil A

pencil B

pencil C

0 cm 1 2 3 4 5 6 7 8 9 10

(a)   Pencil A is about _____ cm long.

(b)   Pencil B is about _____ cm long.

(c)   Pencil C is about _____ cm long.

3. Circle the correct answer.

(a)   The length of a swimming pool is 10 **cm** or **m**.

(b)   My sister is about 90 **cm** or **m** tall.

Complete Worksheet **2** · Page **159 – 162**

Comparing Length in Metres

In Focus

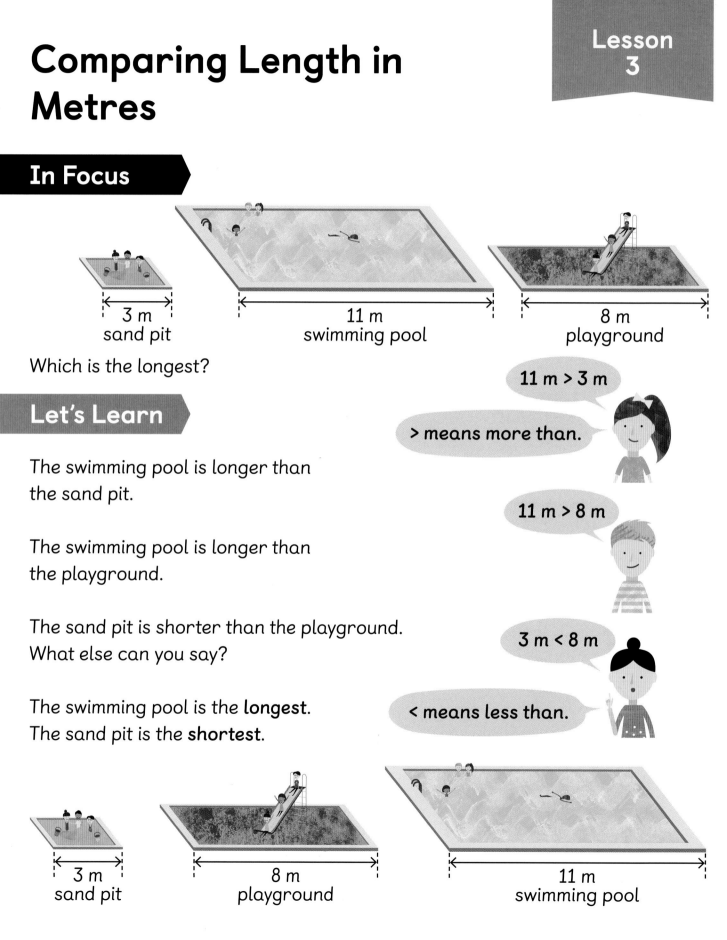

3 m
sand pit

11 m
swimming pool

8 m
playground

Which is the longest?

Let's Learn

The swimming pool is longer than
the sand pit.

The swimming pool is longer than
the playground.

The sand pit is shorter than the playground.
What else can you say?

The swimming pool is the **longest**.
The sand pit is the **shortest**.

11 m > 3 m

> means more than.

11 m > 8 m

3 m < 8 m

< means less than.

3 m
sand pit

8 m
playground

11 m
swimming pool

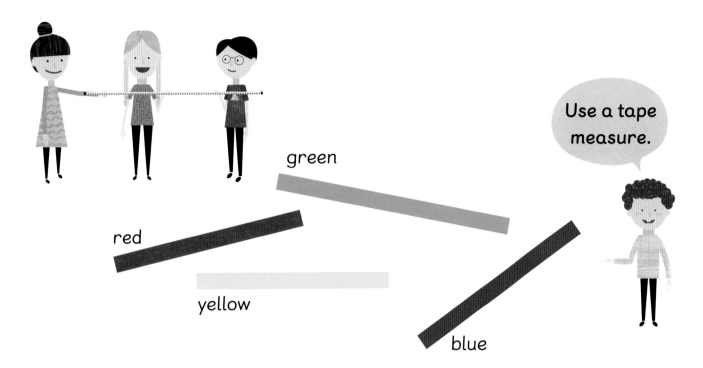

green

red

yellow

blue

Use a tape measure.

Measure the length of the 4 tapes provided by your teacher.

Make sentences to describe what you find.

(a)   The [   ] tape is shorter than the [   ] tape.

(b)   The [   ] tape is longer than the [   ] tape.

(c)   The [   ] tape is the shortest.

(d)   The [   ] tape is the longest.

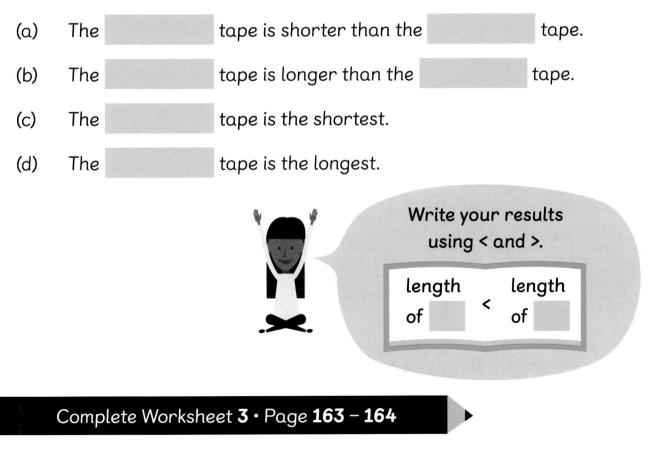

Write your results using < and >.

length of [   ] < length of [   ]

Complete Worksheet 3 · Page 163 – 164

Comparing Length in Centimetres

In Focus

Compare the length of the three things.

Let's Learn

Why do we put the things at the zero mark to compare?

The comb is about 8 cm long.
The crayon is about 6 cm long.
The straw is about 7 cm long.

$8 - 6 = 2$
The comb is about 2 cm longer than the crayon.

$8 - 7 = 1$
The comb is about 1 cm longer than the straw.

The comb is the longest.
The crayon is the shortest.

length of 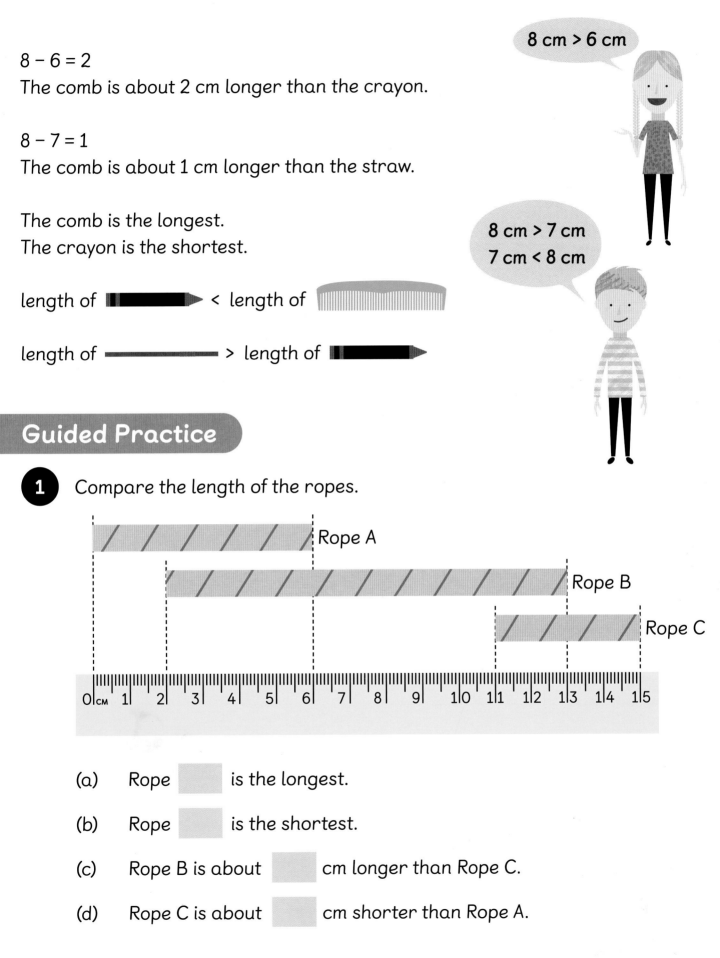 < length of

length of ——————— > length of

8 cm > 6 cm

8 cm > 7 cm
7 cm < 8 cm

Guided Practice

1 Compare the length of the ropes.

Rope A

Rope B

Rope C

0 CM 1 2 3 4 5 6 7 8 9 10 11 12 13 14 15

(a) Rope ▢ is the longest.

(b) Rope ▢ is the shortest.

(c) Rope B is about ▢ cm longer than Rope C.

(d) Rope C is about ▢ cm shorter than Rope A.

2 Compare the length of the presents.

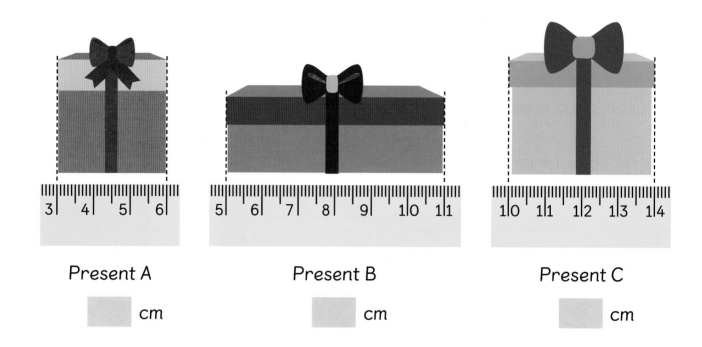

Present A

[ ] cm

Present B

[ ] cm

Present C

[ ] cm

Arrange the presents in order of length.
Start with the longest.

Present [ ] , Present [ ] , Present [ ]

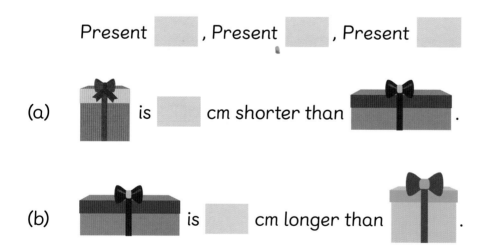

(a) [ ] is [ ] cm shorter than [ ] .

(b) [ ] is [ ] cm longer than [ ] .

3 Compare the height of the presents.

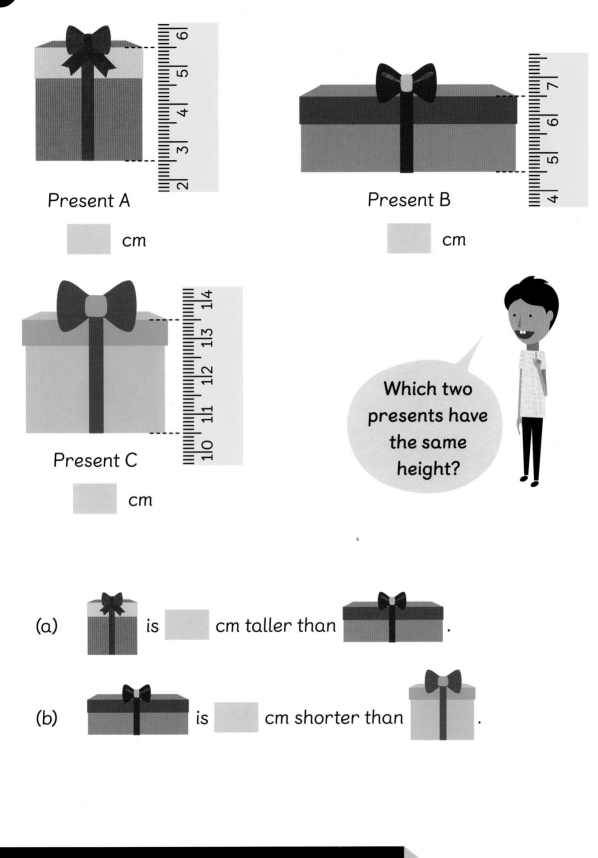

Present A

[   ] cm

Present B

[   ] cm

Present C

[   ] cm

Which two presents have the same height?

(a) [image] is [   ] cm taller than [image].

(b) [image] is [   ] cm shorter than [image].

Complete Worksheet **4** · Page **165 – 166**

Comparing the Length of Lines

In Focus

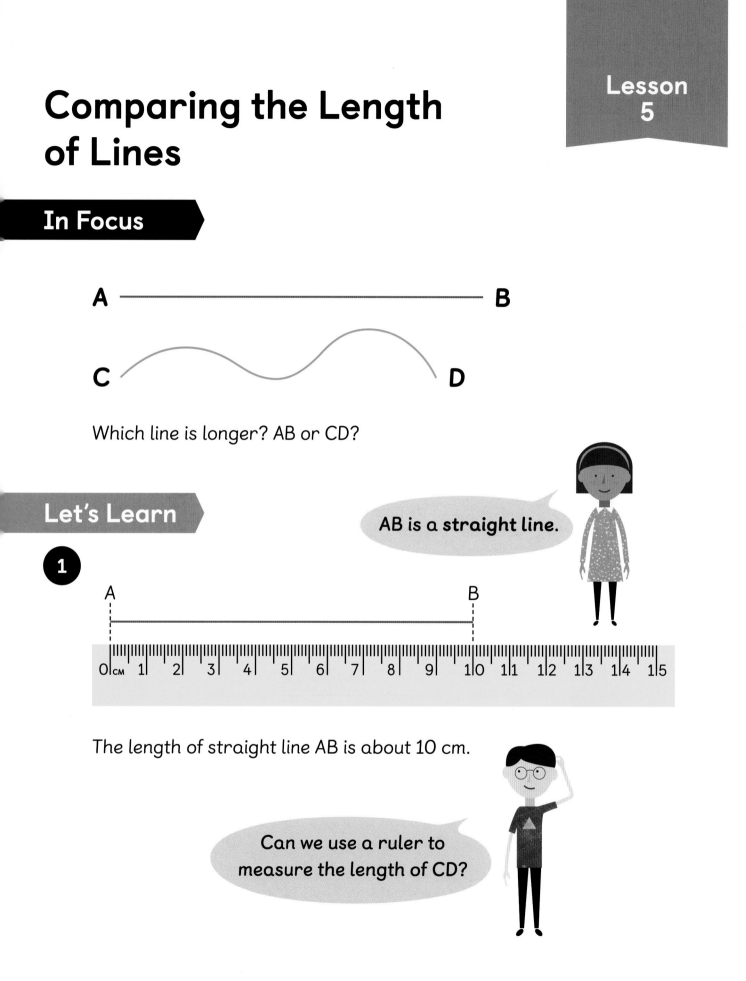

A ——————————————————— B

C〰〰〰〰〰〰 D

Which line is longer? AB or CD?

Let's Learn

AB is a straight line.

1

The length of straight line AB is about 10 cm.

Can we use a ruler to measure the length of CD?

2 We can use a string to measure the length of CD.

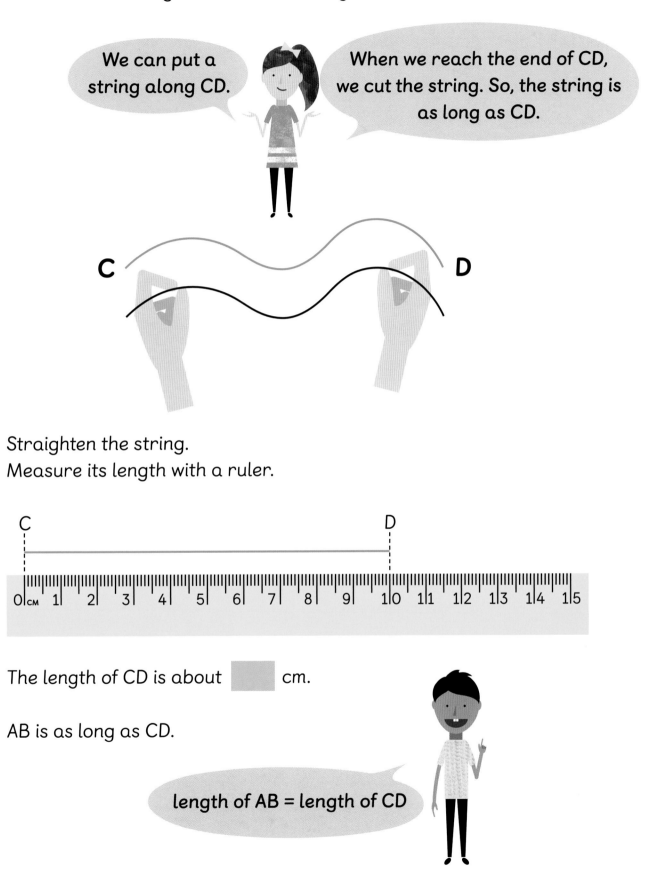

We can put a
string along CD.

When we reach the end of CD,
we cut the string. So, the string is
as long as CD.

C   D

Straighten the string.
Measure its length with a ruler.

C   D

The length of CD is about ⬚ cm.

AB is as long as CD.

length of AB = length of CD

3 Measure and compare.

Line ____ is the longest.

Line RS is about ____ cm longer than line PQ.

Line PQ is about ____ cm shorter than line TU.

Activity Time

Work in pairs.

What you need:

① Using a stick, draw a straight line about 8 cm long.

② Measure each other's line.
   Whose line is closer to 8 cm long?

③ Guess the length of each piece of string shown.

④ Use the [spool] and the [ruler] to measure the length of the strings.

1   Use a ruler to draw each line.

   (a)   Draw a straight line AB that is about 5 cm long.

   (b)   Draw a straight line CD that is about 2 cm longer than AB.

2   Use a string and a ruler.

   (a)   Measure the length of line AB.

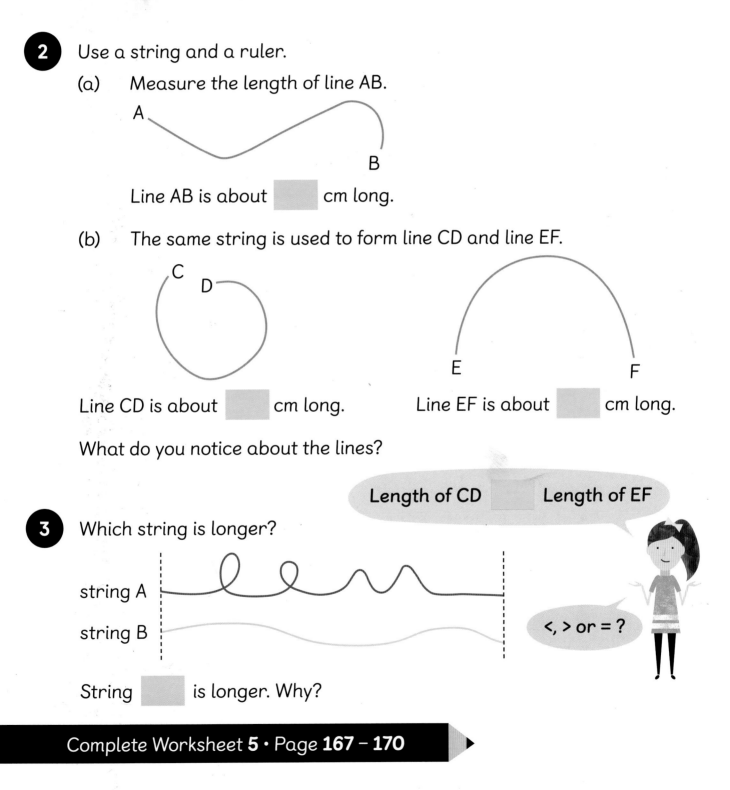

   Line AB is about ⬜ cm long.

   (b)   The same string is used to form line CD and line EF.

   Line CD is about ⬜ cm long.   Line EF is about ⬜ cm long.

   What do you notice about the lines?

   Length of CD ⬜ Length of EF

3   Which string is longer?

   string A

   string B

   <, > or = ?

   String ⬜ is longer. Why?

Complete Worksheet 5 · Page 167 – 170

Solving Word Problems

In Focus

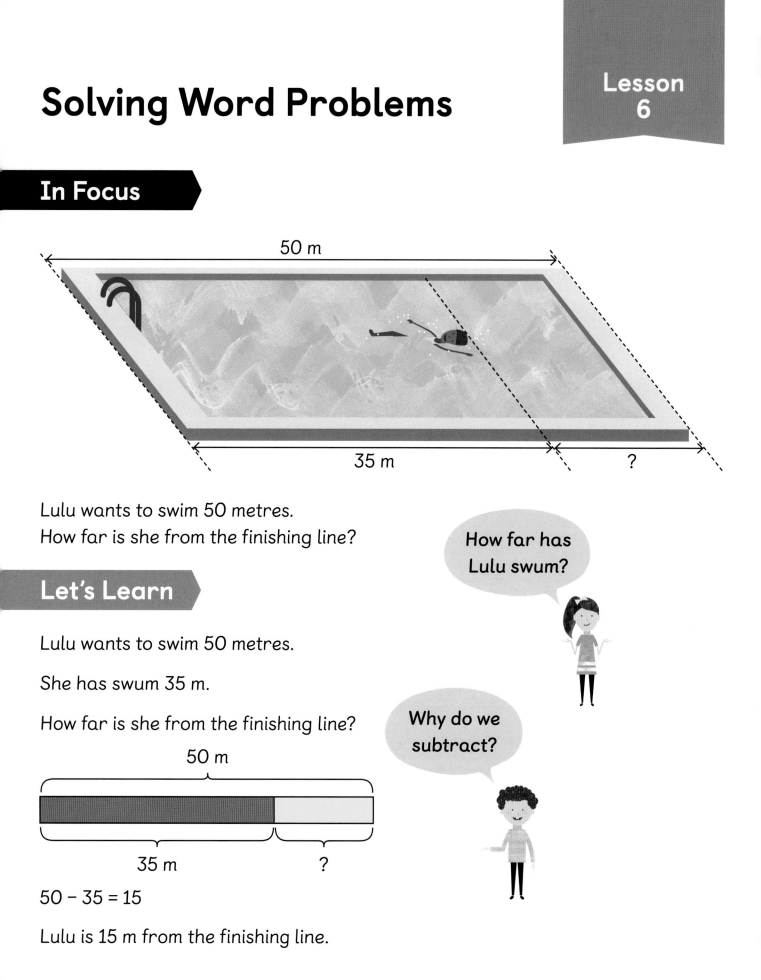

Lulu wants to swim 50 metres.
How far is she from the finishing line?

How far has
Lulu swum?

Let's Learn

Lulu wants to swim 50 metres.

She has swum 35 m.

How far is she from the finishing line?

Why do we
subtract?

$$50 - 35 = 15$$

Lulu is 15 m from the finishing line.

Guided Practice

1 Emma buys 18 m of red cloth and 15 m of blue cloth.
What is the total length of cloth that she buys?

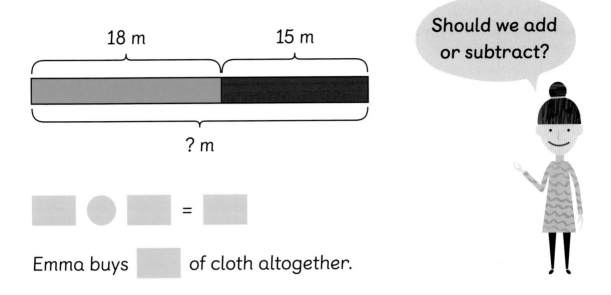

Should we add or subtract?

Emma buys [ ] of cloth altogether.

2 Ruby has a ribbon that is 80 cm long.
She cuts a piece that is 48 cm long to make a bow.
What is the length of ribbon left?

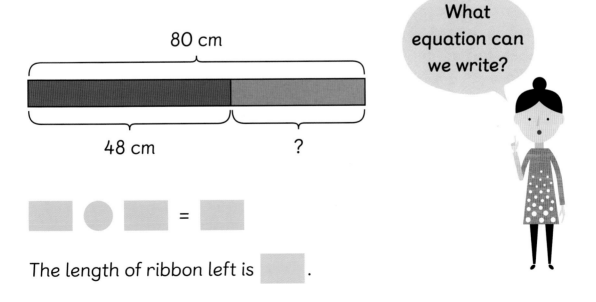

What equation can we write?

The length of ribbon left is [ ].

3 A toy clown is standing on a pair of stilts that are 35 cm high.
The height of the clown when he is standing on the stilts is 99 cm.

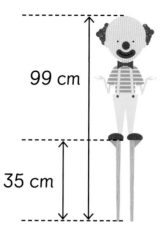

99 cm

35 cm

What is the height of the toy clown?

4 A robot moves from 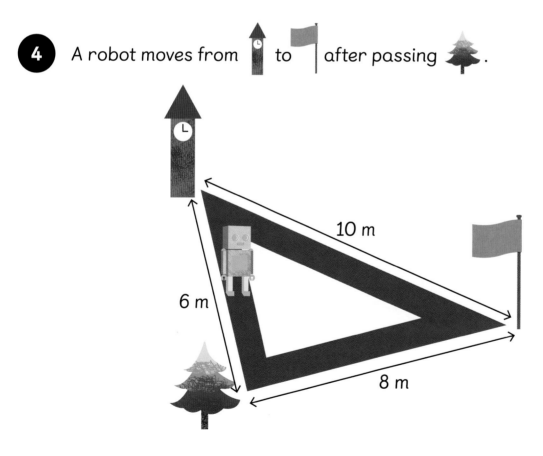 to ⚑ after passing 🌲.

10 m

6 m

8 m

How far does it travel?

Complete Worksheet **6** · Page **171 – 174**

Solving Word Problems

In Focus

Holly sticks 5 stickers in a row.
What is the total length of the row of stickers?

Let's Learn

Elliott's method:

2 cm

$5 \times 2 = 10$
The row of stickers is 10 cm long.

Charles' method

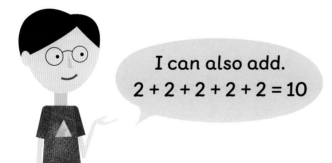

I can also add.
$2 + 2 + 2 + 2 + 2 = 10$

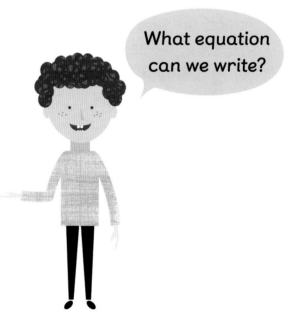

What equation can we write?

The row of stickers is 10 cm long.

1 Ravi stacks 3 identical boxes.
The height of each box is 4 cm.
What is the total height of the stack of boxes?
Solve using two different methods.

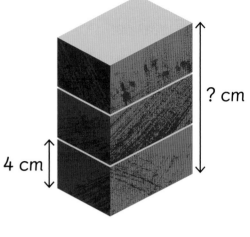

? cm

4 cm

The total height of the stack of boxes is [ ] cm.

2 Amira puts 6 toothpicks in one line.
Each toothpick is 5 cm long.
What is the length of the line of toothpicks?
Solve using two different methods.

The length of the line of toothpicks is [ ] cm.

Complete Worksheet **7** · Page **175 – 176**

Solving Word Problems

In Focus

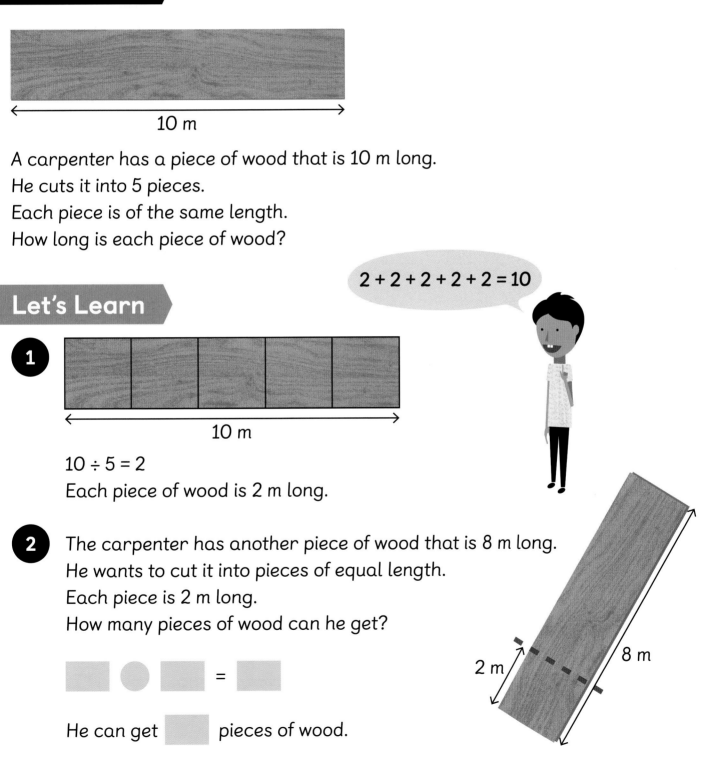

10 m

A carpenter has a piece of wood that is 10 m long.
He cuts it into 5 pieces.
Each piece is of the same length.
How long is each piece of wood?

Let's Learn

2 + 2 + 2 + 2 + 2 = 10

1

10 m

$10 \div 5 = 2$
Each piece of wood is 2 m long.

2 The carpenter has another piece of wood that is 8 m long.
He wants to cut it into pieces of equal length.
Each piece is 2 m long.
How many pieces of wood can he get?

☐ ◯ ☐ = ☐

He can get ☐ pieces of wood.

2 m   8 m

A rope is 20 m long.
It is cut into 10 pieces of equal length.
What is the length of each piece?

The length of each rope is ▢ m.

2 A tailor needs 3 m of cloth to make one dress.
How many dresses can he make with 18 m of cloth?

He can make ▢ dresses.

3 Charles bent a wire that is 12 m long to form a square.
The square has 4 sides of equal length.
How long is each side?

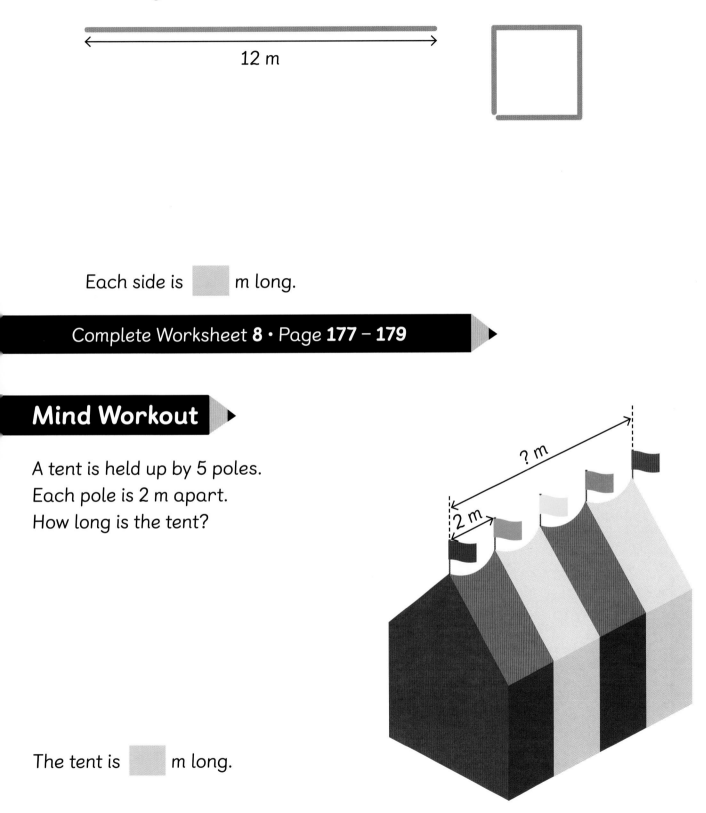

12 m

Each side is ☐ m long.

Complete Worksheet **8** · Page **177 – 179**

Mind Workout

A tent is held up by 5 poles.
Each pole is 2 m apart.
How long is the tent?

? m

2 m

The tent is ☐ m long.

Charles has the longest fishing rod.
Amira's fishing rod is longer than Ravi's fishing rod.
Who has the shortest fishing rod?

Tell your classmates how you solve this problem.

I know how to...

☐ how to measure length in metres (m).

☐ how to measure length in centimetres (cm).

☐ when to use cm or m to measure length.

☐ how to compare and order length.

☐ how to measure and draw lines.

☐ how to solve word problems on length.

How do we find how heavy things are?

Chapter 6
Mass

Measuring Mass in Kilograms

In Focus

We can buy these things by mass.
We can measure mass using a weighing scale.
How do we find how heavy things are?

Let's Learn

1 This is a one-kilogram mass.

The **kilogram** is a unit of mass.
We write **kg** for kilogram.

We can hold objects to feel how heavy they are.

Your teacher will let you hold a one-kilogram mass.

1kg

We usually measure the mass of heavy objects in kilograms.

2 We can use a balance to tell how heavy things are.

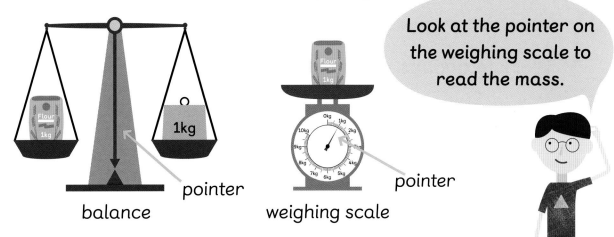

balance   weighing scale

Look at the pointer on the weighing scale to read the mass.

The mass of the packet of flour is about 1 kg.
The packet of flour is **as heavy as** a one-kilogram mass.

3

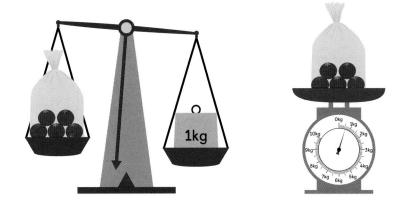

The bag of tomatoes is **lighter than** 1 kg.
The mass of the bag of tomatoes is **less than** 1 kg.

4

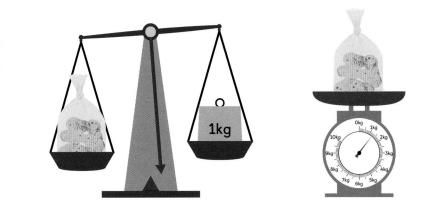

The bag of potatoes is **heavier than** 1 kg.
The mass of the bag of potatoes is **more than** 1 kg.

Work in groups of 4.

What you need:

① Hold the 1kg.
Feel how heavy it is.

② Look for five objects around us.

③ Compare each thing with the 1kg
in your hand.

④ Guess if each thing is heavier
than, lighter than or about 1 kg.

⑤ Use ⏲ to check your guesses.

thing	guess (✓)			check (✓)		
	heavier than 1 kg	lighter than 1 kg	about 1 kg	heavier than 1 kg	lighter than 1 kg	about 1 kg
exercise book		✓			✓	

Which of the things weighs about 1 kg?

Guided Practice

1 Find the mass of the watermelon.

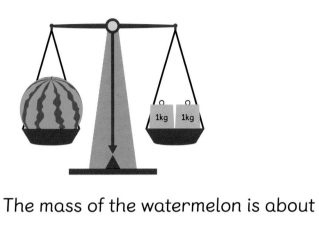

The mass of the watermelon is about ☐ kg.

2 What is the mass of each item?

(a)

(b)

☐ kg

☐ kg

3 Find the mass of the cabbage.

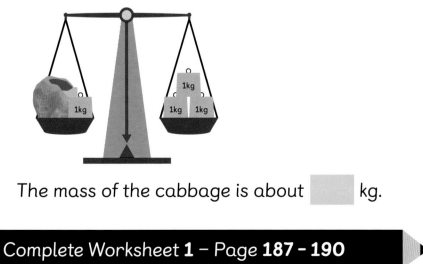

The mass of the cabbage is about ☐ kg.

Complete Worksheet 1 – Page 187 - 190

Measuring Mass in Grams

These things are light.
Do we use kilograms to measure the mass of these things? Why?

Let's Learn

1 This is a one-gram mass. 1g

We use a one-gram mass to measure the mass of lighter objects.

The **gram** is a smaller unit of mass.
We write **g** for gram.

2 Use a balance to measure the mass.

Can you find other objects that have a mass of about 1 g?

The paper clip has a mass of about 1 g.

Work in groups of 4.

What you need:

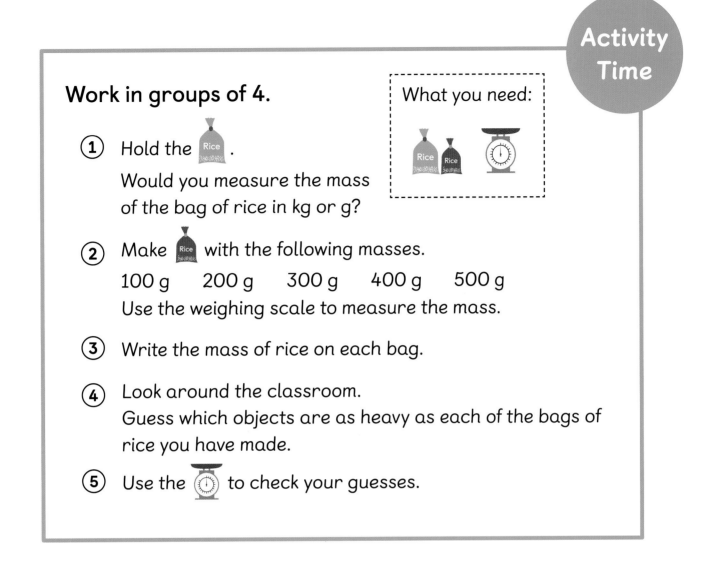

① Hold the 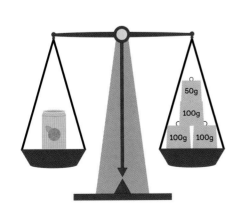 Rice .
Would you measure the mass of the bag of rice in kg or g?

② Make Rice with the following masses.
100 g   200 g   300 g   400 g   500 g
Use the weighing scale to measure the mass.

③ Write the mass of rice on each bag.

④ Look around the classroom.
Guess which objects are as heavy as each of the bags of rice you have made.

⑤ Use the to check your guesses.

Guided Practice

1

The mass of the drink can is about ⬜ g.

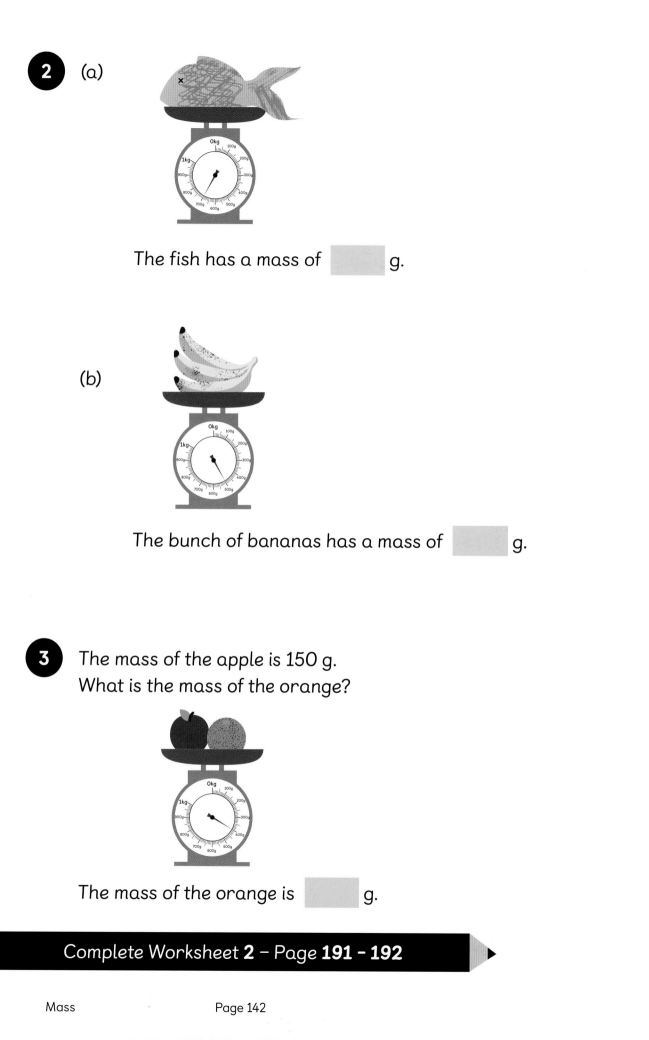

2 (a)

The fish has a mass of ▢ g.

(b)

The bunch of bananas has a mass of ▢ g.

3 The mass of the apple is 150 g.
What is the mass of the orange?

The mass of the orange is ▢ g.

Complete Worksheet **2** – Page **191 – 192**

Measuring Mass in Grams

In Focus

The mass of the mango is about 200 g.
What is the mass of the bag of flour?

Let's Learn

1

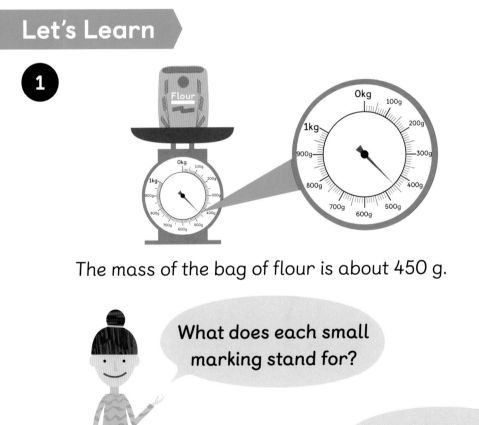

The mass of the bag of flour is about 450 g.

What does each small marking stand for?

Each small marking stands for 10 g.

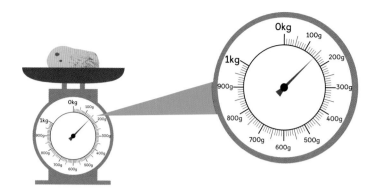

The mass of the potato is about 150 g.

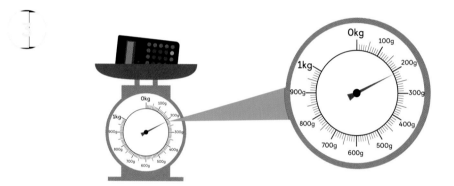

The mass of the calculator is about 210 g.

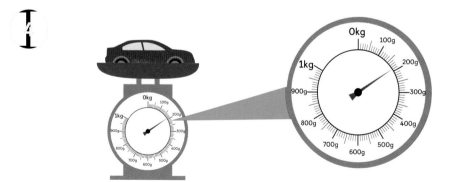

The mass of the toy car is about 190 g.

Work in groups of 4.

What you need:

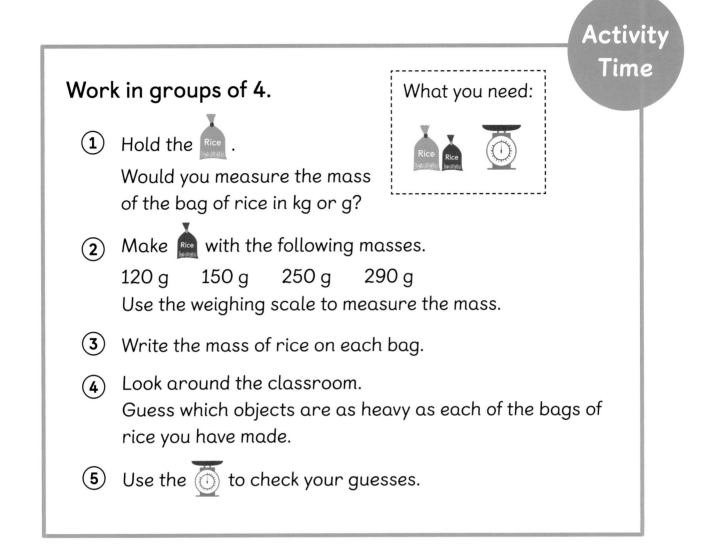

① Hold the Rice .
Would you measure the mass of the bag of rice in kg or g?

② Make Rice with the following masses.
120 g   150 g   250 g   290 g
Use the weighing scale to measure the mass.

③ Write the mass of rice on each bag.

④ Look around the classroom.
Guess which objects are as heavy as each of the bags of rice you have made.

⑤ Use the ⚖ to check your guesses.

Guided Practice

1

The mass of the packet of crisps is about [   ] g.

2 What is the mass?

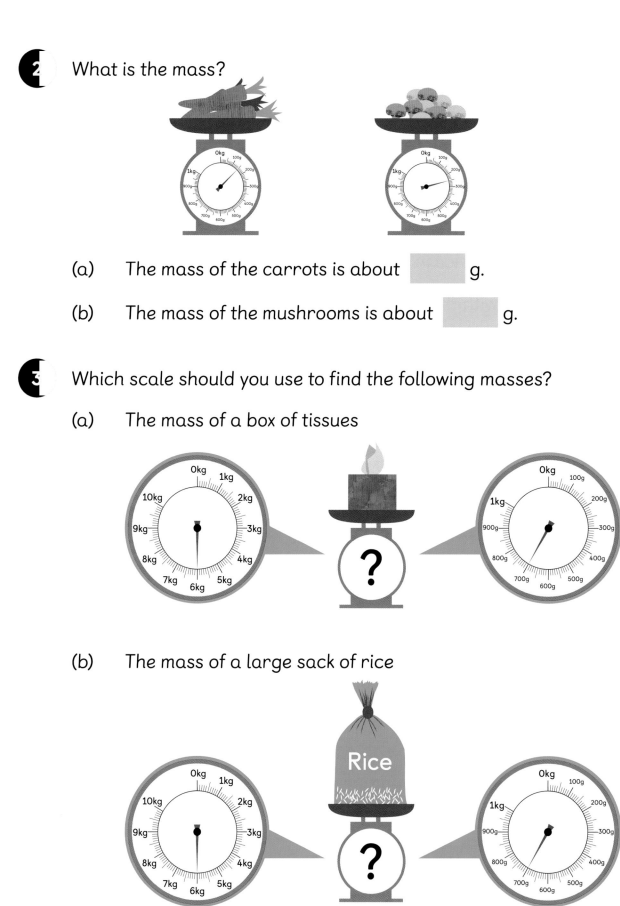

(a)   The mass of the carrots is about [_____] g.

(b)   The mass of the mushrooms is about [_____] g.

3 Which scale should you use to find the following masses?

(a)   The mass of a box of tissues

(b)   The mass of a large sack of rice

Rice

Complete Worksheet **3** – Page **193 – 196**

Comparing Masses of Two Objects

In Focus

How can we tell which box is heavier?

Let's Learn

We can use a weighing scale to measure the mass of each box.

The mass of the green box is about 5 kg.

The mass of the red box is about 2 kg.

The green box is heavier than the red box.
It is 3 kg heavier than the red box.

The red box is lighter than the green box.
It is 3 kg lighter than the green box.

$5 - 2 = 3$

The mass of the green box > the mass of red box.
The mass of red box < the mass of green box.

Work in groups of 4 to 5.

(1) Take turns to use 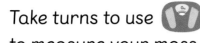 to measure your mass.

name	mass
Amira	about 21 kg

(2) Compare the mass of any 2 pupils.

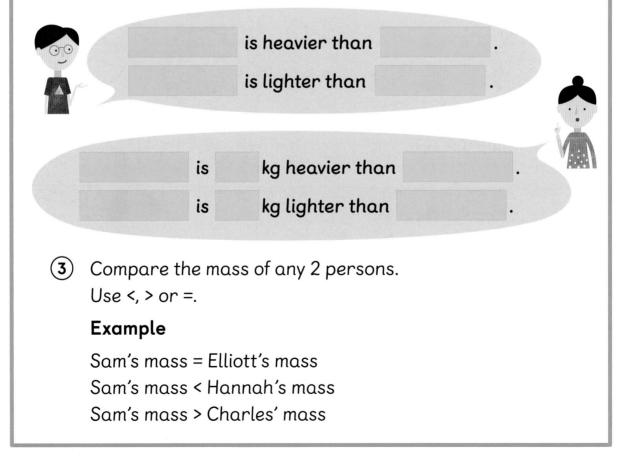

[   ] is heavier than [   ].

[   ] is lighter than [   ].

[   ] is [   ] kg heavier than [   ].

[   ] is [   ] kg lighter than [   ].

(3) Compare the mass of any 2 persons.
Use <, > or =.

Example

Sam's mass = Elliott's mass

Sam's mass < Hannah's mass

Sam's mass > Charles' mass

1. Write the missing numbers.

(a) The mass of the tomato is about [ ] g.

(b) The mass of the carrot is about [ ] g.

(c) The tomato is [ ] g heavier than the carrot.

(d) The carrot is [ ] g lighter than the tomato.

2. Compare the masses of the children.

Ravi

30 kg

Ruby

22 kg

Emma

25 kg

(a) Who is heavier, Ravi or Ruby?

(b) Who is lighter, Emma or Ruby?

(c) Ravi is [ ] kg heavier than Emma.

(d) Ruby is [ ] kg lighter than Ravi.

3 Fill in the blanks with **true** or **false**.

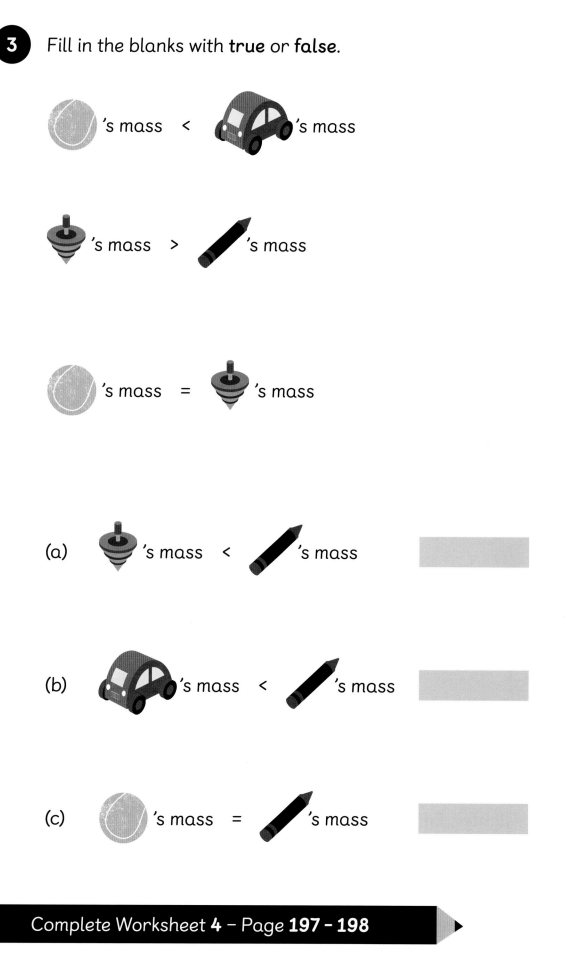

's mass < 's mass

's mass > 's mass

's mass = 's mass

(a) 's mass < 's mass

(b) 's mass < 's mass

(c) 's mass = 's mass

Complete Worksheet **4** – Page **197 – 198**

Comparing the Mass of Three Objects

In Focus

jelly beans

marbles

popcorn

All the jars weigh the same.

How do we compare the masses of the jars?

Let's Learn

The mass of the jar filled with jelly beans is about 320 g.
The mass of the jar filled with marbles is about 490 g.
The mass of the jar filled with popcorn is about 160 g.

490 − 320 = 170
The jar of marbles is 170 g heavier than the jar of jelly beans.

490 − 160 = 330
The jar of marbles is 330 g heavier than the jar of popcorn.

The jar of marbles is the **heaviest**.
The jar of popcorn is the **lightest**.

Arrange the jars from the lightest to the heaviest.

mass of   mass of
>

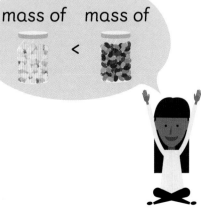
mass of   mass of
<

popcorn	jelly beans	marbles
160 g	320 g	490 g
lightest		heaviest

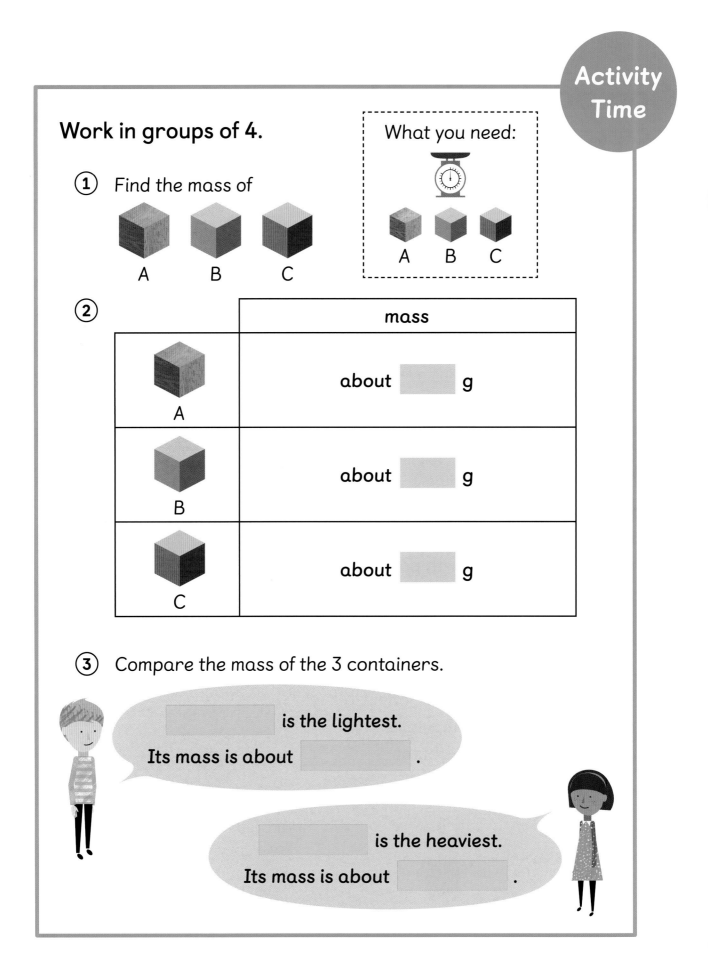

Work in groups of 4.

① Find the mass of

A   B   C

What you need:

A   B   C

②

	mass
A	about ☐ g
B	about ☐ g
C	about ☐ g

③ Compare the mass of the 3 containers.

☐ is the lightest.
Its mass is about ☐ .

☐ is the heaviest.
Its mass is about ☐ .

Guided Practice

1 The mass of sweets is usually measured in grams.

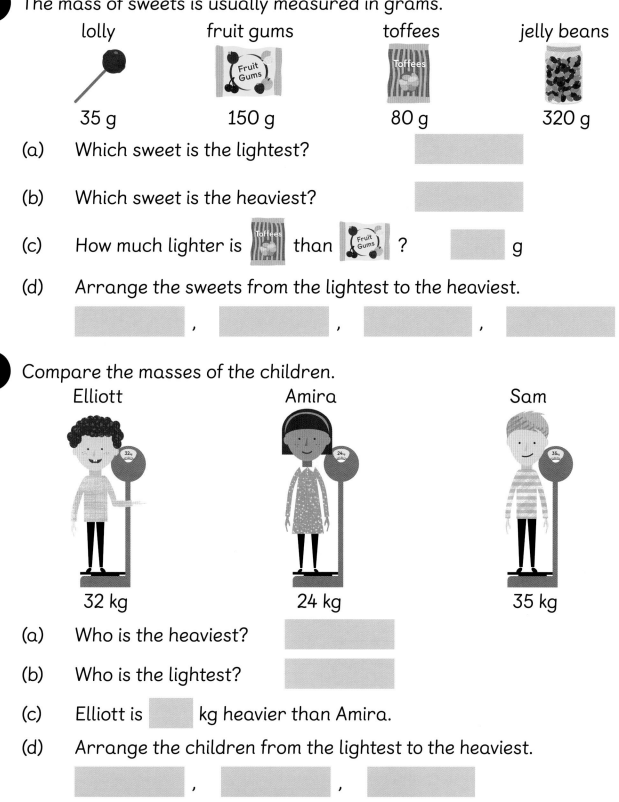

lolly	fruit gums	toffees	jelly beans
35 g	150 g	80 g	320 g

(a)   Which sweet is the lightest?

(b)   Which sweet is the heaviest?

(c)   How much lighter is [Toffees] than [Fruit Gums] ?   g

(d)   Arrange the sweets from the lightest to the heaviest.

        ,   ,   ,

2 Compare the masses of the children.

Elliott   Amira   Sam

32 kg   24 kg   35 kg

(a)   Who is the heaviest?

(b)   Who is the lightest?

(c)   Elliott is   kg heavier than Amira.

(d)   Arrange the children from the lightest to the heaviest.

        ,   ,

Complete Worksheet 5 – Page 199 - 200

Solving Word Problems

In Focus

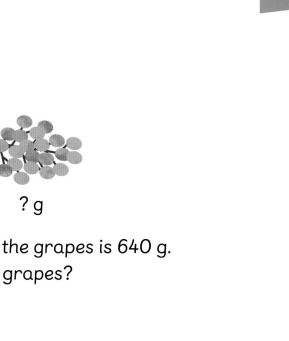

380 g　　　　　　　　? g

The total mass of the bowl and the grapes is 640 g.
How do we find the mass of the grapes?

Let's Learn

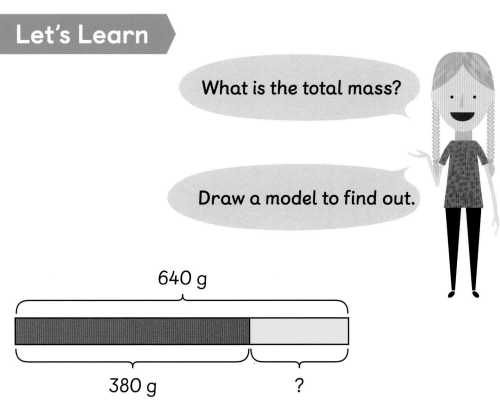

What is the total mass?

Draw a model to find out.

640 g

380 g　　　?

640 − 380 = 260
The mass of the grapes is 260 g.

1 The mass of a pear is 135 g.
A watermelon is 375 g heavier than the pear.
What is the mass of the watermelon?

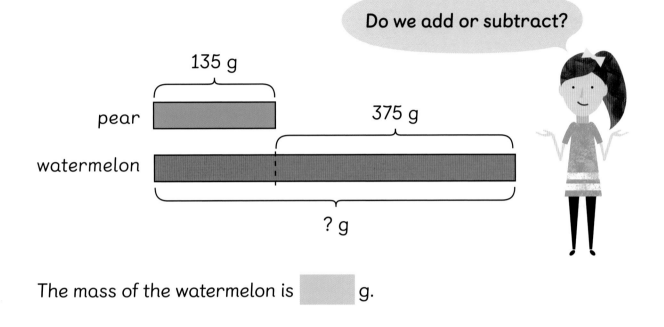

Do we add or subtract?

The mass of the watermelon is ⬚ g.

2 An empty suitcase has a mass of 3 kg.
Charles packs 9 kg of clothes into the suitcase.
He also packs 4 kg of books into the suitcase.
What is the total mass of the suitcase with the clothes and books?

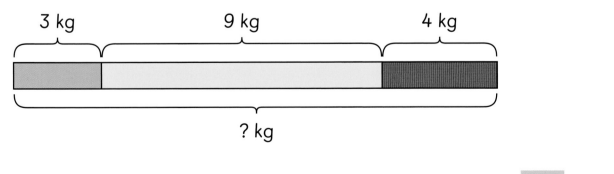

The total mass of the suitcase with the clothes and books is ⬚ kg.

3

loaf of bread   bun

The mass of a loaf of bread is 450 g.
A bun is 125 g lighter than the loaf of bread.
What is the mass of the bun?

4   The mass of 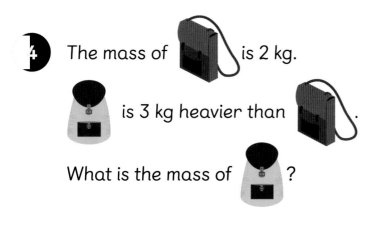 is 2 kg.

is 3 kg heavier than   .

What is the mass of   ?

5   Together, Sam and Ravi weigh 64 kg.
Sam weighs 31 kg.
What is Ravi's mass?

6   There is 2 kg of potatoes in a sack.
Holly adds 7 kg of potatoes to the sack.
Emma puts another 3 kg of potatoes into the sack.
What is the total mass of potatoes in the sack?

Complete Worksheet **6** – Page **201 – 204**

Solving More Word Problems

In Focus

How do we find out the total mass of the 4 bags of rice?

Let's Learn

1 Elliott bought 4 bags of rice.
Each bag has a mass of 3 kg.

3	3	3	3

$4 \times 3 = 12$
The total mass of the 4 bags of rice is 12 kg.

> Another way is to add.
> $3 + 3 + 3 + 3 = 12$

2 The total mass of 5 bags of flour is 40 kg.
Each bag of flour has the same mass.
What is the mass of each bag of flour?

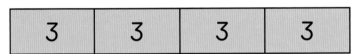

40 kg

$40 \div 5 = 8$
The mass of each bag of flour is 8 kg.

1   What is the mass of each bag of washing powder?

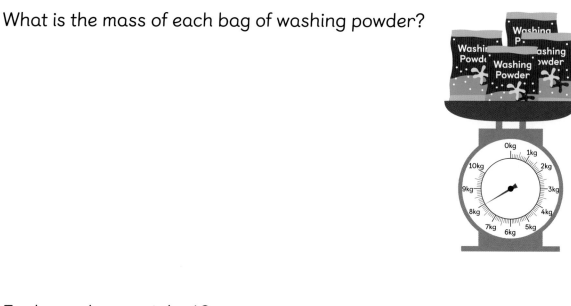

2   Each envelope weighs 10 g.
What is the total mass of 6 identical envelopes?

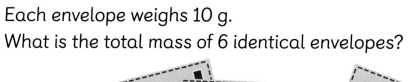

Hannah has 9 coins.
Each coin has a mass of 5 g.
What is the total mass of the coins?

4 A shopkeeper has a few bags of oranges.
The mass of each bag of oranges is 5 kg.
The total mass of the bags of oranges is 35 kg.
How many bags of oranges does the shopkeeper have?

Complete Worksheet **7** – Page **205 - 207**

Mind Workout

Look at the balances.

What can you say about the mass of ?

Weighing scales are used in many places.

Look around when you go shopping with your parents.
Take pictures of the weighing scales that you see.

Show your pictures to your classmates.
Tell them how each weighing scale is used.

I know how to...

☐ measure mass in kilograms (kg).

☐ measure mass in grams (g).

☐ compare and order mass.

☐ solve word problems on mass.

Do you know what a thermometer is?

Chapter 7
Temperature

Reading Temperature

In Focus

This cup of water feels warm.

What happens when we put a thermometer into warm water?

Let's Learn

1

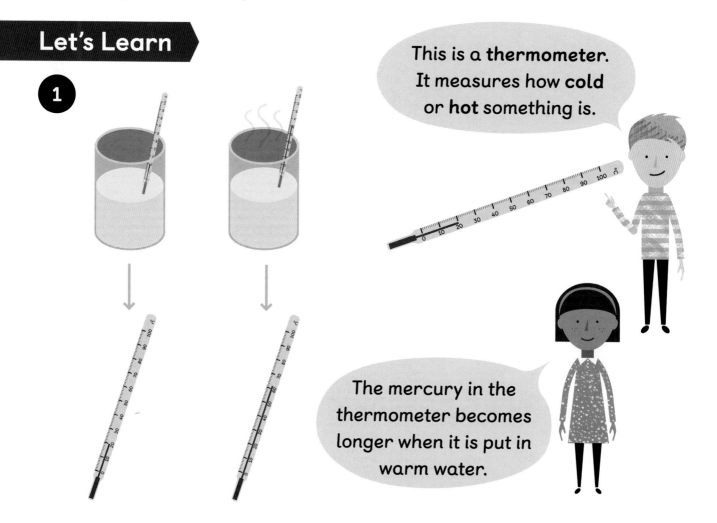

This is a **thermometer**. It measures how **cold** or **hot** something is.

The mercury in the thermometer becomes longer when it is put in warm water.

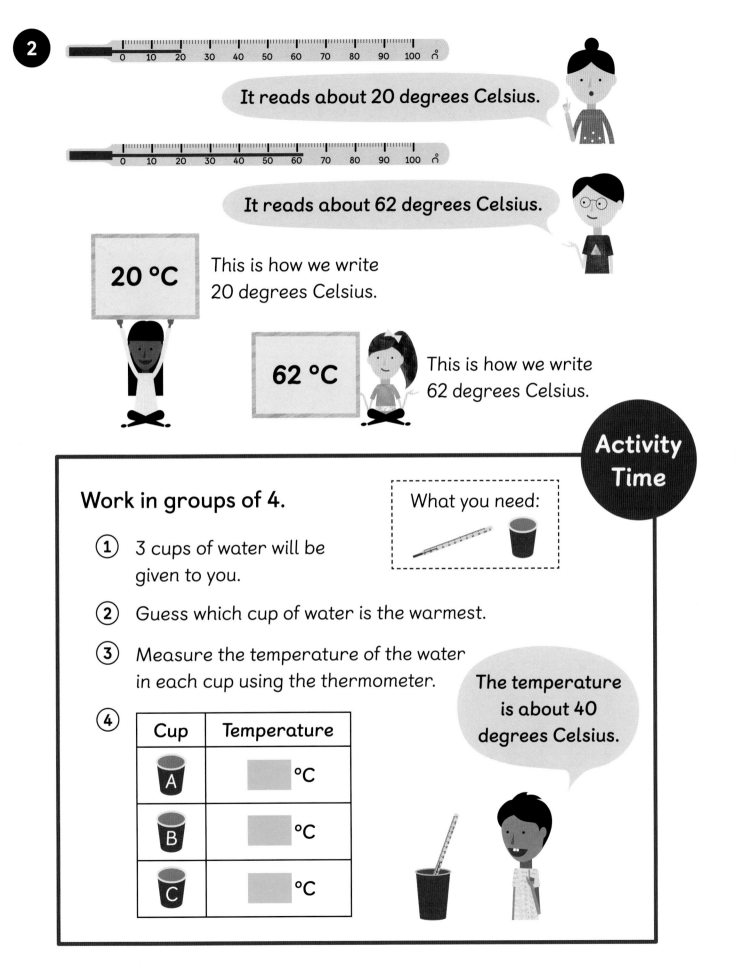

2

It reads about 20 degrees Celsius.

It reads about 62 degrees Celsius.

20 °C This is how we write 20 degrees Celsius.

62 °C This is how we write 62 degrees Celsius.

Activity Time

Work in groups of 4.

What you need:

① 3 cups of water will be given to you.

② Guess which cup of water is the warmest.

③ Measure the temperature of the water in each cup using the thermometer.

The temperature is about 40 degrees Celsius.

④

Cup	Temperature
A	°C
B	°C
C	°C

1 Write the missing numbers.

(a)

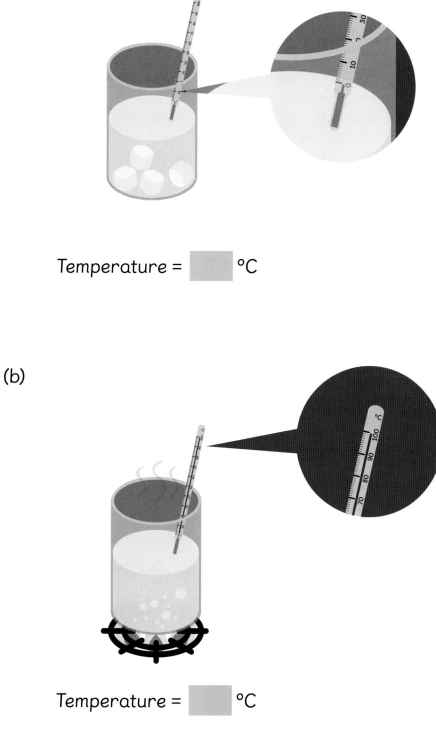

Temperature = ☐ °C

(b)

Temperature = ☐ °C

2 Sam mixes different amounts of hot water with tap water in various cups.
He measures the temperature of the water.
What is the temperature of the water in each cup?

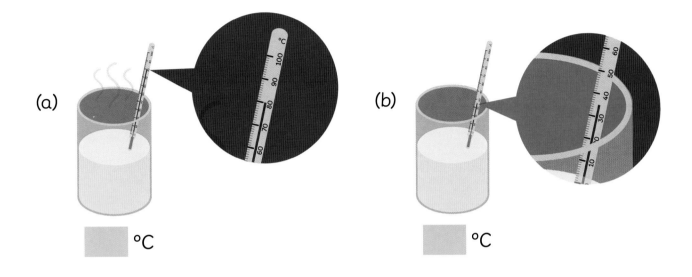

(a) ⬚ °C

(b) ⬚ °C

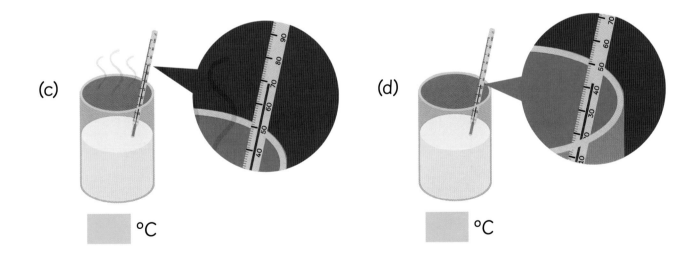

(c) ⬚ °C

(d) ⬚ °C

Complete Worksheet **1** – Page **215 – 219**

Estimating Temperature

In Focus

What is the temperature today?
Is it a warm day?

Let's Learn

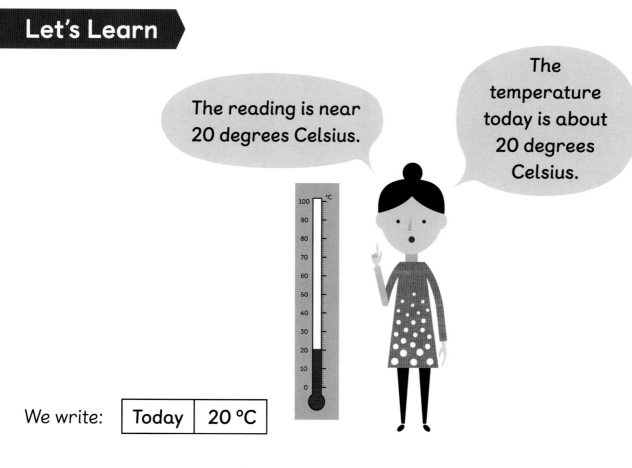

The reading is near 20 degrees Celsius.

The temperature today is about 20 degrees Celsius.

We write:

Today	20 °C

Work in pairs.

① For 5 days, read the thermometer each day to see the temperature.

② Record and compare the readings with your partner.

What you need:

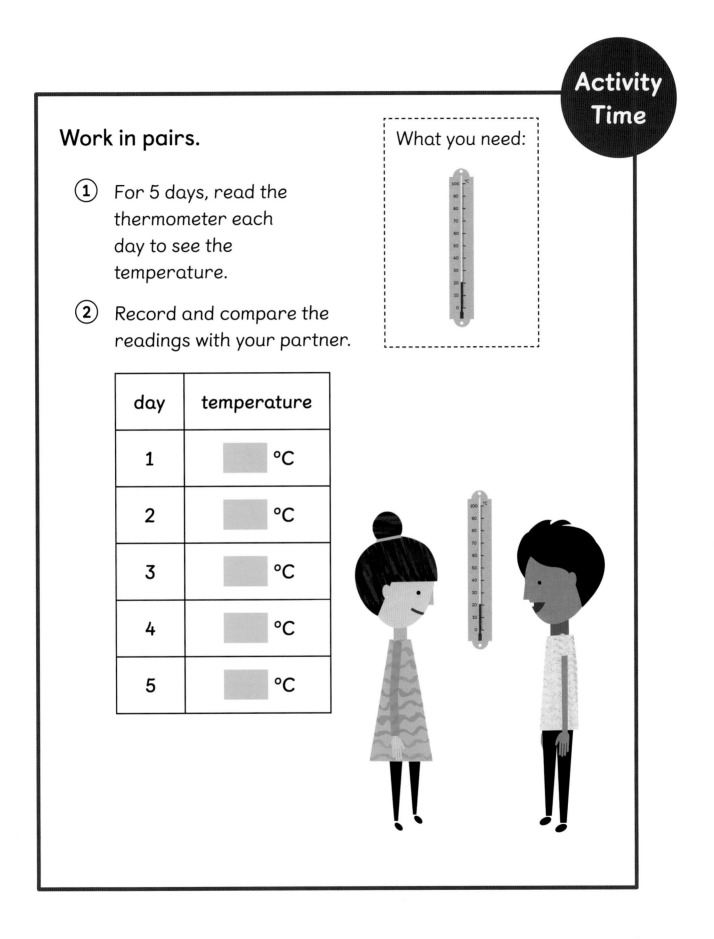

day	temperature
1	°C
2	°C
3	°C
4	°C
5	°C

1 Estimate the temperatures.

(a)

[   ] °C

(b)

[   ] °C

(c)

[   ] °C

(d)

[   ] °C

2 Estimate the temperatures.

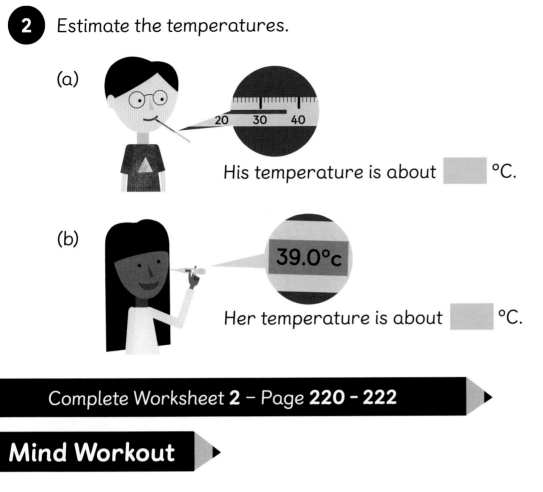

(a)

His temperature is about ▢ °C.

(b)

39.0°c

Her temperature is about ▢ °C.

Complete Worksheet **2** – Page **220 – 222**

Mind Workout

Elliott checked the temperature outside his house at a certain time on Monday. He did the same every day for another 4 days.

| 13 °C | 17 °C | 23 °C | 21 °C | 16 °C |

(a)   The highest temperature was on Thursday.

(b)   The lowest temperature was on Monday.

(c)   The temperature on Wednesday was more than 20 °C.

(d)   The temperature on Friday was less than the temperature on Tuesday.

What was the temperature each day?

Monday	Tuesday	Wednesday	Thursday	Friday
▢ °C	▢ °C	▢ °C	▢ °C	▢ °C

Hot

Cool

Cold

Warm

Write down one temperature for each word.
Copy the thermometer in your journal.
Colour to show each temperature.

Example

Lulu's Journal

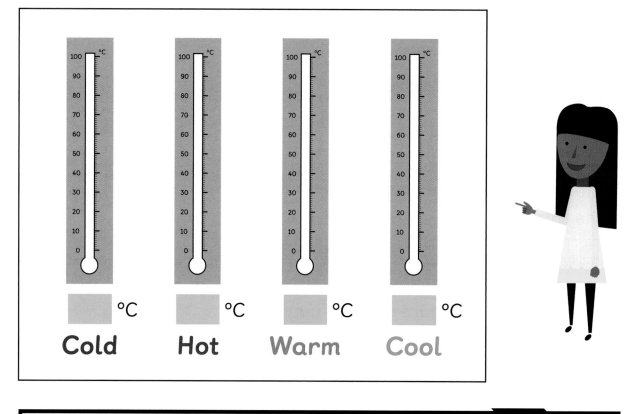

°C Cold

°C Hot

°C Warm

°C Cool

I know how to...

☐ read a thermometer.

☐ measure and write down the temperature.

Self Check

How many stars does each group have?

Chapter 8
Picture Graphs

Reading Picture Graphs

In Focus

Group D

Which is easier to count? Why?

Let's Learn

1 This is a **picture graph**. It shows the number of stars each group has.

A picture graph is also called a pictogram.

The title tells us what the picture graph shows.

Class 1H's Reward Chart

Group	Stars	Number of stars
A	★★★★★★★★	8
B	★★★	3
C	★★★★★★★★	8
D	★★★★★★★★★	9

Group D has the **most** number of stars.
Group B has the **least** number of stars.
Group A has **as many** stars **as** Group C.

Work in groups of 4.

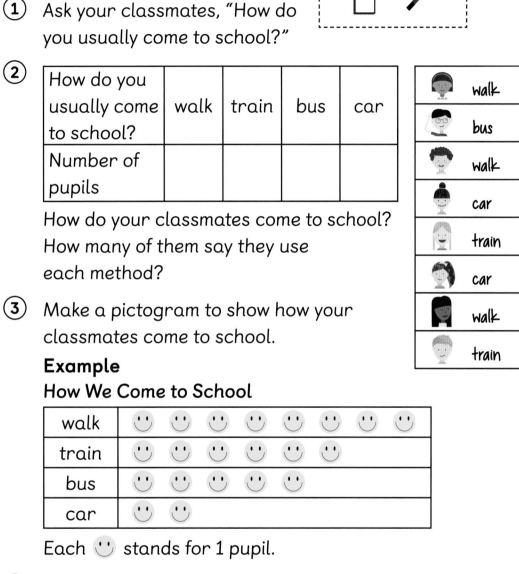

What you need:

① Ask your classmates, "How do you usually come to school?"

②

How do you usually come to school?	walk	train	bus	car
Number of pupils				

How do your classmates come to school? How many of them say they use each method?

③ Make a pictogram to show how your classmates come to school.

Example
How We Come to School

walk	☺ ☺ ☺ ☺ ☺ ☺ ☺ ☺
train	☺ ☺ ☺ ☺ ☺ ☺
bus	☺ ☺ ☺ ☺ ☺
car	☺ ☺

Each ☺ stands for 1 pupil.

④ Write 5 sentences about the pictogram.
Use words such as **more than, fewer than, most, least** and **as many as.**

⑤ Ask your classmates to check your sentences.

Complete Worksheet **1** – Page **229 - 232**

Reading Picture Graphs

In Focus

The pictogram shows the number of sweets four children have.

Sweets the Children Have

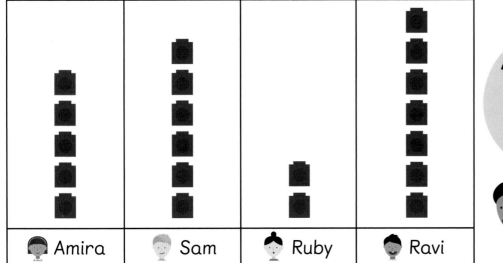

Each  stands for 1 sweet.

Describe the number of sweets the four children have.

Amira has 5 sweets.
Sam has 6 sweets.
Ruby has 2 sweets.
Ravi has 7 sweets.

Let's Learn

This is a table.

	Amira	Sam	Ruby	Ravi
Number of sweets	5	6	2	7

Amira has 3 **more** sweets than Ruby.
Sam has 1 **fewer** sweet than Ravi.
Ravi has the **greatest** number of sweets.
Ruby has the **smallest** number of sweets.
They have 20 sweets in all.

Work in pairs.

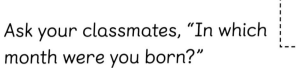

What you need:

① Ask your classmates, "In which month were you born?"

② Count and show using /.
Each / stands for 1 pupil.

Month	Jan	Feb	Mar	Apr	May	Jun	Jul	Aug	Sep	Oct	Nov	Dec
Number of pupils												

③ Make a chart using /.

Example

Our Birthday Month

January to March	////
April to June	/////
July to September	///// //
October to December	///// /////

This is a **tally chart**.

Guided Practice

The tally chart and pictogram show the number of fruits in a basket.

Fruits in the Basket

strawberry	~~////~~ /
orange	//
pear	////
apple	~~////~~ //

Fruits in the Basket

| strawberry | orange | pear | apple |

Each picture stands for one piece of fruit.

(a)   How many strawberries are there?

(b)   There are [   ] oranges.

(c)   There are [   ] pears.

(d)   How many apples are there?

(e)   The number of [   ] is the greatest.

(f)   There is [   ] more apple than strawberries.

(g)   How many fruits are there in the basket altogether?

Fruits in the Basket

strawberry	orange	pear	apple

Each 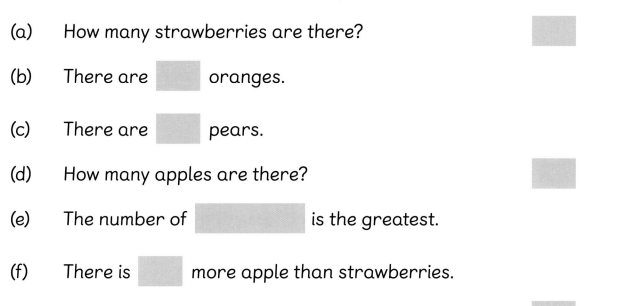 stands for one piece of fruit.

Make a pictogram for the number of fruits in the basket using ▮ .

Complete Worksheet **2** – Page **233 – 236**

Reading Picture Graphs

In Focus

The pictogram shows the number of each type of animal that Charles sees in the zoo.

Animals in the Zoo

Each ⬤ stands for 1 animal.

How can Charles show the pictogram on a tally chart and a table?

Let's Learn

1 Charles shows the pictogram on a tally chart and a table.

Animals in the Zoo

tiger	giraffe	elephant	monkey
//// ////	/////	//	//// /

Animal	Number of animals
tiger	10
giraffe	4
elephant	2
monkey	6

2 We can also use one ● to stand for 2 animals.

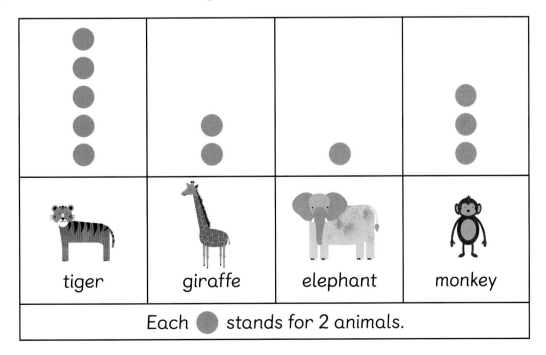

Each ● stands for 2 animals.

(a)

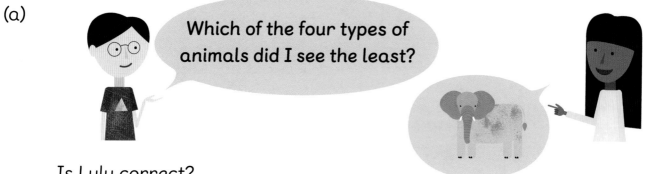

Which of the four types of animals did I see the least?

Is Lulu correct?

There are 10 tigers, 4 giraffes, 2 elephants and 6 monkeys.
Charles saw the fewest elephants.

Lulu is correct.

(b)   Is Elliott correct?

Each ● stands for 2 animals.
There are 2 elephants.

Elliott is not correct.

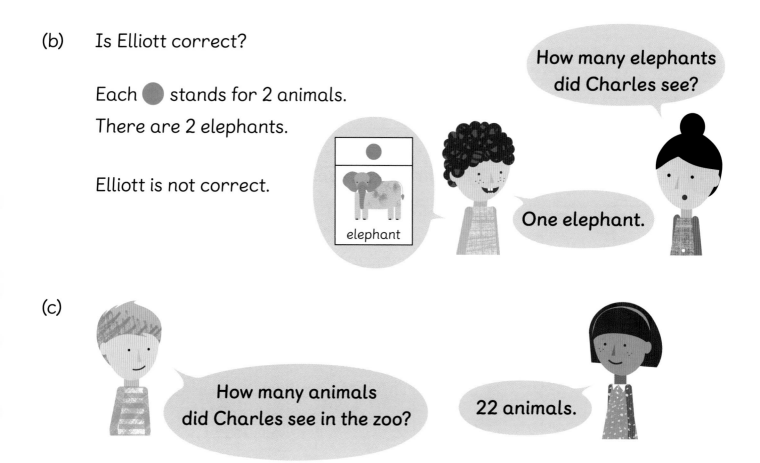

How many elephants did Charles see?

elephant

One elephant.

(c)

How many animals did Charles see in the zoo?

22 animals.

Is Amira correct?

Method 1

Animal	Number of ●	Number of animals
tiger	5	10
giraffe	2	4
elephant	1	2
monkey	3	6

Total = 10 + 4 + 2 + 6
        = 22

Method 2

There are 5 + 2 + 1 + 3 = 11 ●.

Each ● stands for 2 animals.

There are 22 animals.

Amira is correct.

3

5 or fewer	more than 5

Which animals belong to this group?

Can you ask other questions that can be answered by looking at the pictogram?

Complete Worksheet 3 – Page **237 – 240**

Reading Picture Graphs

In Focus

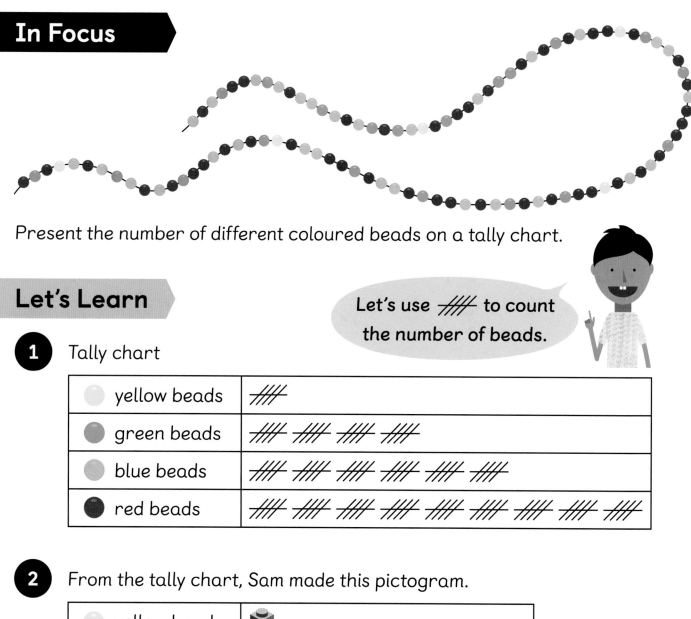

Present the number of different coloured beads on a tally chart.

Let's Learn

Let's use 卌 to count the number of beads.

1 Tally chart

🟡	yellow beads	卌
🟢	green beads	卌 卌 卌 卌
🔵	blue beads	卌 卌 卌 卌 卌 卌
🔴	red beads	卌 卌 卌 卌 卌 卌 卌 卌 卌

2 From the tally chart, Sam made this pictogram.

🟡	yellow beads	🧊
🟢	green beads	🧊🧊🧊🧊
🔵	blue beads	🧊🧊🧊🧊🧊🧊
🔴	red beads	🧊🧊🧊🧊🧊🧊🧊🧊🧊

Each 🧊 stands for 5 beads.

Ruby also made this pictogram.

⚪ yellow beads	🟫 🟫 🟫 🟫 🟫
🔘 green beads	🟫 🟫 🟫
⚪ blue beads	🟫 🟫 🟫 🟫 🟫
⚫ red beads	🟫 🟫 🟫 🟫 🟫 🟫 🟫 🟫

Each 🟫 stands for 5 beads.

Who made a mistake in making the pictogram, Sam or Ruby?

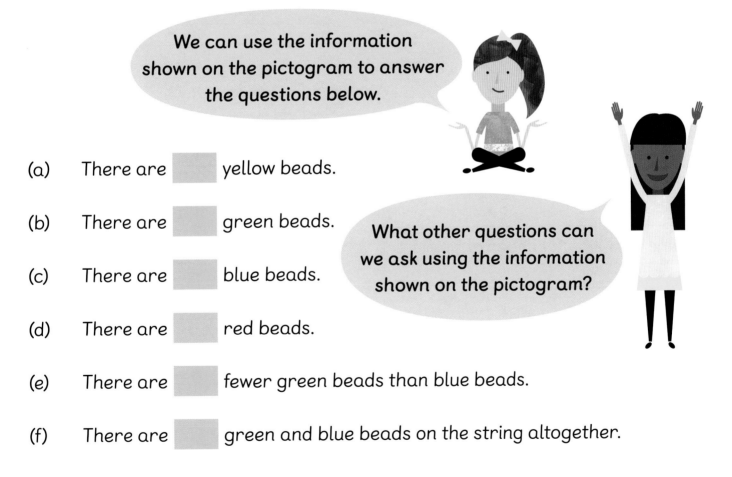

We can use the information shown on the pictogram to answer the questions below.

(a)   There are ☐ yellow beads.

(b)   There are ☐ green beads.

(c)   There are ☐ blue beads.

(d)   There are ☐ red beads.

What other questions can we ask using the information shown on the pictogram?

(e)   There are ☐ fewer green beads than blue beads.

(f)   There are ☐ green and blue beads on the string altogether.

Complete Worksheet 4 – Page **241 – 244**

Reading Picture Graphs

In Focus

The tally chart and table shows the number of books four boys read last year.

Books We Read

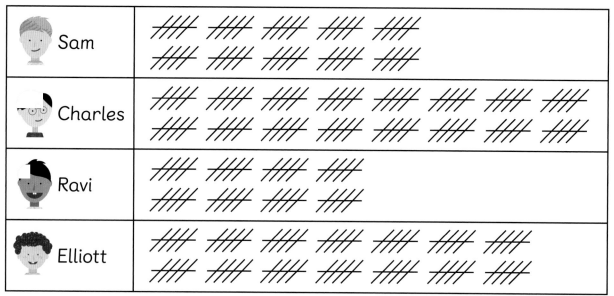

Name	Number of books
Sam	50
Charles	80
Ravi	40
Elliott	70

Make a pictogram to show the number of books each boy read.

Let's Learn

The pictogram shows the number of books each boy read last year.

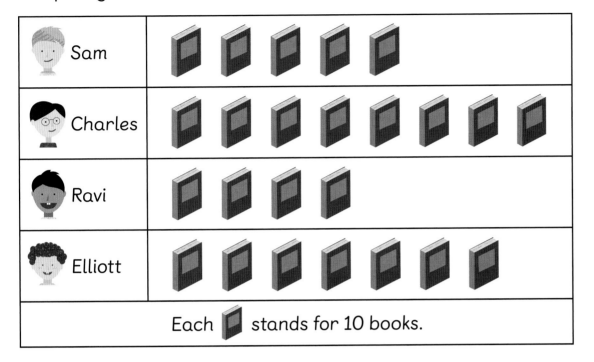

Each 📖 stands for 10 books.

(a)   How many books did Elliott read?

(b)   Who read the most books last year?

(c)   Who read the fewest books last year?

(d)   How many fewer books did Sam read than Charles?

(e)   How many more books did Charles read than Ravi?

(f)   How many books did Sam and Ravi read altogether?

I read 75 books last year.
How can I show the number of books
I read on the pictogram?

Guided Practice

Ask questions that can be answered using the information in the pictogram.

Pupils Who Wear Glasses

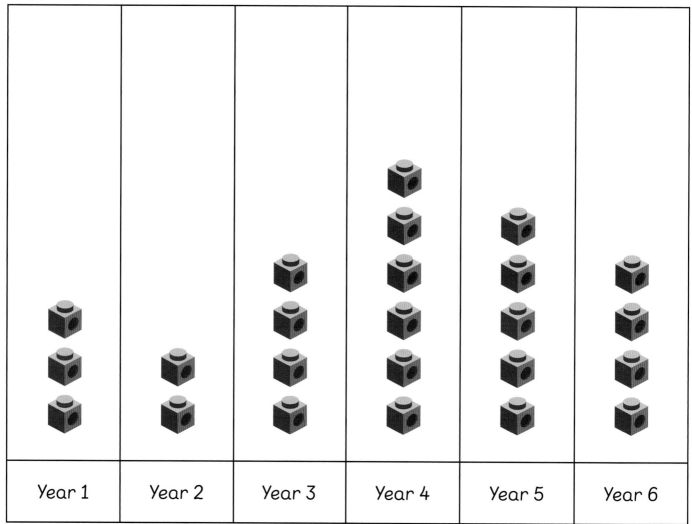

Each stands for 10 pupils.

Complete Worksheet **5 – Page 245 - 247**

Mind Workout

Elliott has 20 red, blue, yellow and green marbles.

He has 3 more red marbles than blue marbles.

He has 9 green marbles.

Complete the pictogram.

Elliott's Marbles

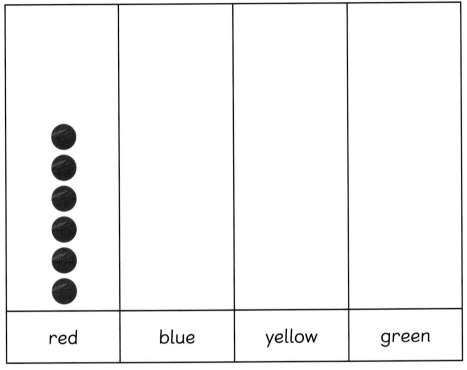

Each ● stands for 1 marble.

(a)   Elliott has [ ] blue marbles.

(b)   Elliott has [ ] yellow marbles.

(c)   Elliott has the most number of [ ] marbles.

(d)   Elliott has the least number of [ ] marbles.

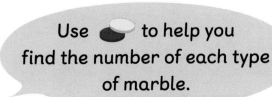

Is there another way to draw the pictogram?

Use ● to help you find the number of each type of marble.

Maths Journal

Look for pictograms in newspapers or magazines.
Show them to your classmates.
Tell your classmates what is shown in each pictogram.

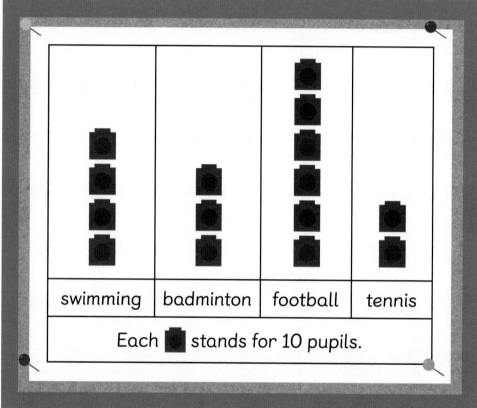

| swimming | badminton | football | tennis |

Each ⬛ stands for 10 pupils.

I know how to...

Self Check

☐ read information from pictograms, block diagrams, tally charts and tables.

☐ make pictograms, block diagrams, tally charts and tables.

☐ solve problems using information from pictograms, block diagrams, tally charts and tables.